GW01445055

OUTCOMES

SPLIT **B** EDITION

INTERMEDIATE
STUDENT'S BOOK

HUGH DELLAR
ANDREW WALKLEY

Split Edition A

1 FIRST CLASS

- say more about yourself and other people
- ask and answer common questions
- ask follow-up questions and maintain conversations
- describe how well you use different languages
- pay more attention to the language in texts
- tell better stories

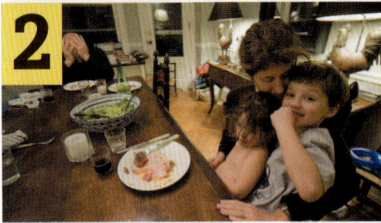

2 FEELINGS

- talk about how you feel – and why
- respond to good and bad news
- talk about your life now
- explain why you can't – or don't want to – do things

VIDEO 1: Kenya comes to Central Park   REVIEW 1   WRITING 1: Keeping in touch

3 TIME OFF

- describe places and explain where they are
- give and respond to suggestions
- discuss future plans
- talk about the weather
- recognise and reuse useful chunks of language
- ask and talk about holiday experiences

4 INTERESTS

- talk about free-time activities
- describe how often you do (or did) things
- explain how good you are at things
- talk about injuries and sports problems
- ask about tastes

VIDEO 2: World Heritage quiz   REVIEW 2   WRITING 2: Short emails

5 WORKING LIFE

- talk about jobs and what they involve
- comment on people's experiences
- discuss rules and freedoms at work
- talk about getting used to changes
- say longer chunks better

6 BUYING AND SELLING

- talk about phones and phone companies
- compare products
- describe what people are wearing
- discuss shopping habits
- describe souvenirs and presents
- negotiate a good price

VIDEO 3: Wheelin' and dealin' antiques   REVIEW 3   WRITING 3: Stories

7 EDUCATION

- describe courses, schools, teachers and students
- show you believe or sympathise with what people tell you
- talk about different education systems
- talk about possible future plans or situations
- discuss different aspects of education
- form and say different words from the same root

8 EATING

- describe different dishes and ways of cooking food
- explain what is on a menu
- discuss experiences of foreign food
- make generalisations
- describe restaurants

VIDEO 4: The business of cranberries   REVIEW 4   WRITING 4: Making requests

GRAMMAR	VOCABULARY	READING	LISTENING	DEVELOPING CONVERSATIONS
• Auxiliary verbs • Narrative tenses	• Talking about people • Talking about languages	• The Google translators in human form	• Meeting for the first time • Stories connected to speaking a foreign language	• Asking follow-up questions
• Linking verbs • Present simple and present continuous	• Feelings • **Understanding vocabulary:** -ed / -ing adjectives	• It only takes Juan Mann to change the world!	• Talking about feelings • Juan Mann • Bumping into an old school friend	• Response expressions
• Future plans • Present perfect simple	• Places of interest • Weather • **Understanding vocabulary:** Useful chunks in texts	• Kraków: Places to visit • Is disaster tourism such a total disaster?	• Visiting Kraków • Holiday plans	• Giving and responding to suggestions
• Habit and frequency • Present perfect continuous and past simple for duration	• Free-time activities • Injuries and problems • Describing music	• The playlist of your life	• Free-time activities • Hidden talent	• *Are you any good?* • Talking about tastes
• *Must* and *can't* for commenting • Talking about rules	• Describing jobs • Work rules and laws • **Understanding vocabulary:** *Be used to* and *get used to*	• Terrible jobs not a thing of the past	• Talking about work • Rules at work	• *Doing what?*
• Comparisons • Noun phrases	• Smartphones • Clothes and accessories • Describing souvenirs and presents	• Shop till you drop!	• In a phone shop • Talking about gifts	• Avoiding repetition • Negotiating prices
• Future time clauses • Zero and first conditionals	• Describing courses • Education • **Understanding vocabulary:** Forming words	• What works in education	• Talking about a course • Talking about education	• *I can imagine, I bet*, etc.
• Generalisations and *tend to* • Second conditionals	• Describing food • Restaurants	• Food for thought	• In a Peruvian restaurant • Talking about restaurants	• Describing dishes

Contents **3**

Split Edition B

IN THIS UNIT YOU LEARN HOW TO:

9 HOUSES

- describe flats, houses and areas
- explain how big places are
- discuss social and economic changes
- compare the past and now
- ask about house rules

page 6

10 GOING OUT

- talk about exhibitions, films and the theatre
- explain exactly where places are
- discuss nights out
- use idioms connected to different parts of the body
- describe different kinds of events
- talk about plans that failed to happen and explain why

page 14

VIDEO 5: One woman's choice page 22   **REVIEW 5:** page 23   **WRITING 5:** Formal emails page 78

11 THE NATURAL WORLD

- tell and participate in telling stories
- describe animals
- show emotions through pronunciation
- talk about challenges and achievements
- discuss natural resources and the economy

page 24

12 PEOPLE I KNOW

- describe character
- talk about your friends and family
- explain how people you know are similar
- talk about memories
- express regrets
- talk about relationships

page 32

VIDEO 6: Greatest journey page 40   **REVIEW 6:** page 41   **WRITING 6:** Reports page 80

13 JOURNEYS

- talk about journeys
- explain travel problems
- discuss immigration
- reflect on past events
- use extreme adjectives to make descriptions more interesting
- talk about problems and whose fault they are

page 42

14 TECHNOLOGY

- talk about computers
- explain and sort out problems
- describe games
- discuss issues around computer gaming
- talk about apps and gadgets

page 50

VIDEO 7: Air pollution tracking page 58   **REVIEW 7:** page 59   **WRITING 7:** Opinion-led essays page 82

15 INJURIES AND ILLNESS

- talk about injuries and illness with a doctor
- discuss health myths and facts
- talk about causes and results
- tell stories about accidents
- report what people said

page 60

16 NEWS AND EVENTS

- talk about types and sources of news
- comment on the news
- use reporting verbs to report news
- describe famous people and events
- discuss issues around fame

page 68

VIDEO 8: Bee therapy page 76   **REVIEW 8:** page 77   **WRITING 8:** Reviews page 84

GRAMMAR	VOCABULARY	READING	LISTENING	DEVELOPING CONVERSATIONS
• Present perfect simple and present perfect continuous • Comparing now and the past	• Describing homes • Social issues • Describing areas	• Waiting for the bubble to burst • Small ads	• A new apartment • Room to rent in Berlin	• Explaining how big a place is • Asking about rules
• Quantifiers • The future in the past	• Exhibitions, films and theatre • **Understanding vocabulary:** Idioms • Describing events	• Big night out	• Going to the cinema • What did you do last night?	• Explaining where places are
• Past ability / obligation • Passives	• Movements and sounds • Challenges and achievements	• The strange story of Maurice Wilson • Natural resources fact file	• Animal stories • Maurice Wilson • The resource curse	• Helping people to tell stories
• *Used to, would* and past simple • Expressing regret using *wish*	• Describing character • Relationships	• Struggling to fit into the role of granny	• Talking about family • Talking about Nicolas	• *That's like …*
• Third conditionals • *Should have*	• Ways of travelling and travel problems • **Understanding vocabulary:** Phrasal verbs • **Understanding vocabulary:** Extreme adjectives	• The long journey to a new life	• Talking about journeys • Holiday problems	• *How come?* • Blaming people
• Articles • Infinitive and -*ing* forms	• Computers • Describing games • Apps and gadgets	• My life as a gamer	• IT help desk • The gaming industry • Totally great or total rubbish?	• Sorting out problems
• Adverbs • Reported speech	• Injuries and illness • **Understanding vocabulary:** Word endings and word class • Accidents and health problems	• Fact or myth?	• At the hospital • Accident on holiday	• Short questions with *any*
• Reporting verbs • Defining relative clauses	• News • Explaining who people are	• Seeking fame and fortune	• Talking about news stories • Talking about famous people	• Introducing and commenting on news

Grammar reference   pages 86–96   Information files   pages 97–98   Audio scripts   pages 99–109

Contents   **5**

9

HOUSES

- describe flats, houses and areas
- explain how big places are
- discuss social and economic changes
- compare the past and now
- ask about house rules

SPEAKING

1 Work in pairs. Discuss the questions.

- Where do you think this photo was taken? Why?
- What do you think would be good / bad about living in a place like this? Think about:
  - the house
  - where it is
  - the local facilities
  - the people who live there
  - the way of life
- Would you like to live there? Why? / Why not?

HOME SWEET HOME

VOCABULARY Describing homes

1 Label the picture with these words.

wood floor	garage	swimming pool
patio	gas central heating	open fire
back garden	balcony	attic
tiled floor	roof terrace	basement

2 Work in groups. Discuss the questions.

- Which of the things in Exercise 1 do you have where you live?
- Of the things you don't have, which two would you most like? Why?
- Which two things could you most easily live without?
- Which things make the biggest difference to the price of a house / flat in your country?

3 Match the sentences (1–10) with the follow-up comments (a–j).

1 It's lovely and **bright** in the summer.
2 It's nice and **compact**.
3 It's very **central**.
4 It's very **convenient** for transport.
5 It's very **spacious**.
6 The rent's very **affordable**.
7 I'm renting a room in a **shared apartment**.
8 I live in a **newly-built** apartment block.
9 It's quite **cramped** with four of us living there.
10 It's quite old and **run-down**.

a It's the biggest place I've ever lived in by a long way!
b I don't need that much space and it's easy to keep clean.
c I'm only paying €80 a week plus bills.
d Luckily, I get on OK with the five other students.
e I can walk into town in ten minutes.
f I mean, it's only a two-bedroom flat and there's only one bathroom.
g It's great – and obviously I don't need to do any work on it!
h It faces south, so we get a lot of sunlight.
i We'll need to do some work on it.
j There's a station five minutes' walk away and several buses go into town.

4 Work in pairs. Discuss which of the words in bold in Exercise 3 describe where you live. Explain why.

8

LISTENING

5 ▶ **41** Listen to two people – Gavin and Lynn – talking about their friends' new apartment. Answer the questions.

1 Why did Nick and Carol move?
2 What is nice about their new place?
3 What are the problems with the new place?

6 ▶ **41** Listen again and complete the sentences with two words in each space.

1 Did I tell you I _____ to see Nick and Carol the other day?
2 I haven't seen them _____ .
3 They said _____ 'hello' to you.
4 That must be nice for them now the kids are _____ .
5 They wanted _____ for the kids.
6 It's on the _____ of an old block.
7 It has got _____ , though.
8 I must go round and see them _____ .

7 Work in groups. Discuss the questions.

• How many times have you moved in your life? Why?
• Have you ever done any work on your place? What?
• Have you ever shared a room? How was it?

PRONUNCIATION

8 ▶ **42** Listen to six phrases said slowly. They all have an added /j/ sound to make it easier to move from one vowel sound to another. Practise saying the phrases in the same slow way. Then practise saying them as quickly as you can.

DEVELOPING CONVERSATIONS

Explaining how big a place is

We often explain the size of places by comparing them with things both speakers know, including the room we are in. We may also point and use gestures. Look at the patterns we often use:

*The front room is huge. It's **about twice the size of** this room.*

*It's got a great kitchen. It's **a similar size to** yours – **maybe a bit** bigger.*

*Her garden's nice. It's **about the size of** mine. / It's **about the same size as** mine.*

*Their bathroom is enormous. It's **about from that wall over there to here**, I guess.*

9 Correct the mistakes in these sentences. You may need to add extra words.

1 His bedroom's tiny. It's about half size of this room.
2 The kitchen is huge. It's three times the size of my.
3 The bathroom's OK. It's about same size as yours – maybe a little bit bigger.
4 They've got a huge garden. It's twice the size of your.
5 They've got a small basement. It's a similar size of this room – maybe a bit smaller.
6 They've got a lovely front room. It's twice as wide as this room and maybe a little bit more long.
7 It's not that big – maybe about from here where that desk is.

10 Think of how large the different rooms in your house / apartment are compared with the room you are in now. Then work in groups. Share your ideas, using the patterns in the box.

CONVERSATION PRACTICE

11 Work in pairs. You are going to roleplay a conversation like the one you heard in Exercise 5. Together, invent a person and details about their new home. Think about the following:

• the location: where they live, who with, when they moved there, and why
• the best / worst things about where they live
• the size of the place – and of the individual rooms
• the local area and facilities

12 Now work with a new partner and roleplay the conversation. Start by asking *Did I tell you I went round to see … the other day?* When you have finished, change roles and have another conversation.

🎥 17 To watch the video and do the activities, see the DVD ROM.

HOUSING BUBBLE

SPEAKING

1 Work in pairs. Discuss the questions.

- What age would you normally expect to do the following things? Does your partner agree?
  - leave home
  - meet your partner for life
  - buy a home
  - earn a good salary
  - start a family
- Do you think the average age to do these things has changed in your country? Since when? In what way?

READING

2 Read this article from 2015 about housing in the UK and China. Then work in pairs. In what ways are the situations in the UK and China similar to your country now or in the past? In what ways are they different?

3 Work in pairs. Decide if the sentences below are about the UK, China or both. Read again and check your answers.

1 Many young people don't have the money to buy a home even if they're working.

2 Property prices have risen quickly in the last year.

3 There aren't enough places for people to live.

4 In general, people prefer not to live too close to others.

5 Wages are generally increasing for middle-class people.

6 A lot of foreign people are buying property as an investment.

7 The current situation will probably change soon because of economic reasons.

8 Many people try to stop big building projects near where they live.

4 Work in groups. Discuss the questions.

- What do you think of the following solutions to the problems talked about in the article? What consequences might there be to each of these solutions?
  - Let house prices crash.
  - Make it more difficult for foreigners to buy housing.
  - Let poor people live in empty homes for free or at a discount.
  - If houses are empty for more than six months, the government can take them.
  - The government gives money to help young people buy a home.
- Can you think of one more solution?
- How much do house prices vary in your town / city / country? Where is the best place to buy?
- If you could live anywhere you wanted, where would you choose? Why?

VOCABULARY Social issues

5 Complete the sentences with these words and phrases.

climate change	cost of energy	house prices
immigration	crime rate	divorce rate

1 The sharp rise in _____ is **largely because of** the economic problems in nearby countries.

2 I heard the increase in the _____ **is mainly due to** conflicts going on in oil-producing regions.

3 The fact that couples work such long hours **may have something to do with** the high _____ .

4 _____ **must have something to do with** all this recent strange weather.

5 The sharp fall in _____ **has something to do with** the fact that banks are lending less money.

6 The _____ is going down **due to** better policing and the fact that the economy is doing well.

WAITING FOR THE
BUBBLE TO BURST

Priced out of the market

Li Jian is a 28-year-old salesman from Guangzhou, China. He is a member of China's growing middle class, who are highly educated and in good jobs with rising salaries, but who cannot afford to buy a home. Property prices in China have been rising steadily for over a decade and the price of a home is currently 25 times the average wage. Li Jian is frustrated by the situation:

'It's impossible for me to buy a home now. I will need the help of my parents, but I also need to find a wife and that's not easy if all I can offer is life in a tiny apartment. I have seen one or two places on sale with a discount, so maybe now the market is beginning to slow down, but then that is a new problem. When do you know the market has hit the bottom? I don't want to buy somewhere and find it's worth less a year later!'

The Shanghai building boom

GRAMMAR

Present perfect simple and present perfect continuous

The present perfect simple and the present perfect continuous can be used to talk about changes or trends from some time in the past to now.

6 Look at these sentences from the article. Then work in pairs and answer the questions below.

a *Property prices in China **have been rising** steadily for over a decade.*

b *Over the last year prices **have increased** sharply.*

c *I **have seen** one or two places on sale with a discount.*

1 Which two phrases show a period of time when the change took place?

2 Can both the present perfect simple and continuous be used with these phrases?

3 Why is the continuous used in sentence a)?

4 Which of the two forms is used to show finished events before now?

G Check your ideas on page 86 and do Exercise 1.

7 Write sentences about trends using the prompts below and a word from each box.

Population / 57 to 60 million / 10 years

The population has been rising gradually over the last ten years.

fall	go down	rise	go up

gradually	slightly	dramatically	a lot

1 The crime rate / 250,000 to 170,000 / twenty years

2 Unemployment / 8% to 15% / two years

3 House prices / down 27% / year

4 The birth rate / down from 2.4 to 1.9 / ten years

5 The average wage / up €2 / three years

6 Petrol prices / up one dollar a litre / two months

G For further practice, see Exercise 2 on page 86.

SPEAKING

8 Think of four social or economic changes that have taken place in your country. Then work in groups. Discuss the changes you thought of. Use some of the phrases in bold in Exercise 5 to say what caused them.

Economics correspondent **Tim Gordon**   **January 29 2015**

A worldwide problem

China is not alone in experiencing problems with house prices. From London to Seoul and Oslo to Taipei, young people in work are finding that their opportunities in life are being limited by high housing costs. Research in the UK has found a growing gap between reality and people's expectations for 'life goals'. In general, young people expect to earn £30,000 a year by the time they're 31. However, over 70% fail to reach this target. Interestingly, even when they do, most people can still not afford to buy the house of their dreams because property prices have risen so much faster than wages. It is, therefore, not surprising that although the average person expects to leave home before they're 22, nearly 10% of adults aged between 30 and 34 still live with their parents. Similarly, while most people hope to have found love by the age of 25, one third are actually still single 15 years later.

Hope in a crash

So what hope is there for people like Li Jian? Well, there are people who believe that the best hope is for the property bubble to burst. Some believe that the current high price of real estate is not good for standards of living or the economy and with over 20% of all homes in China's urban areas currently empty, it is entirely possible that prices could crash in the near future.

Protesting to preserve the Englishman's castle

Cultural barriers to change

In the UK, the problem is different. There is a shortage of housing which generally keeps prices high and over the last year prices have increased sharply – to 15 times the average income. The problem is particularly bad in London, where investors from abroad are buying huge amounts of property. However, there are also cultural attitudes that prevent change. Take, for instance, the saying 'An Englishman's home is his castle.' As it suggests, many people in the UK like their space and privacy and will fight for it. As such, most buyers prefer to own a house with a garden, rather than live in an apartment block. Finally, when there are plans to build new large blocks, many local people often protest, to protect their homes from the shadows of large buildings and the increased people, noise and traffic they bring. Without a change of attitudes, falling house prices are less likely than in China.

ROOM TO RENT

SPEAKING

1 Work in pairs and look at the photos of Berlin. What do you know about the city?

2 Read the adverts for six host families for foreign students studying in Berlin. Rank them from 1 (= best) to 6 (= worst) according to your opinion.

Close to U-Bahn underground station.

8km from the city centre – near airport, Lake Tegel and woodlands. Huge and beautifully decorated house. This very friendly family offers half board (€260) or self-catering (€190) accommodation.

BRIGHT APARTMENT

in the up-and-coming area of Friedrichshain. Self-catering rooms for two single students sharing with a friendly lady owner. Relaxed atmosphere. Within walking distance of lively nightlife. (€180)

COMPACT ROOM
with access to own kitchen facilities. Large old house owned by a retired couple offering quiet, comfortable accommodation. Very central. (€220)

This cheerful household consists of a young couple, two-year-old boy and baby. Breakfast and evening meal included. Lovely, spacious room in a flat in smart residential area near Tiergarten Park and embassies. (€290)

Beautiful country house

in village 35km from Berlin. Very green! Young and friendly homeowner. Internet access. 15 minutes to train station. (€170 with breakfast)

Good-sized room

in lovely big apartment. A 45-minute bus ride from the centre. A very pleasant family of four (children 16 and 20). The flat is beautifully decorated. Half board (very good cuisine). Two dogs. Non-smoking girls only. (€200)

3 Work in groups. Discuss the order you chose and why.

VOCABULARY Describing areas

4 Complete the descriptions of areas in a city with these words.

rough	isolated	connected	smart
dead	multicultural	filthy	lively

1 There are a lot more bars and restaurants than there used to be, so it's quite _____ at night now.

2 There's a lot of crime and quite a few social problems, so it's a bit _____ .

3 A lot of immigrants have settled there so it's a lot more _____ than it was in the past.

4 It used to be a fairly cheap, working class place, but it's become a very _____ residential area – and very expensive!

5 It's in the middle of nowhere. You basically need a car or you'll be a bit _____ .

6 The streets are _____ . They're covered in litter and there's graffiti everywhere.

7 There's absolutely nothing to do around there so it's pretty _____ at night. There isn't even a café.

8 It's better _____ than it was thanks to the new tram line.

5 Write a list of areas you know. Then work in pairs. Swap your papers and ask *What's X like?* Answer using language from Exercise 4.

LISTENING

6 ▶ **43** Listen to a conversation between an English man, Shola, and a German woman, Anastasia, who has a room to rent. Work in pairs and discuss the questions.

1 Which of the places in Exercise 2 is he visiting?

2 Do you think he'll rent the room? Why? / Why not?

7 ▶ **43** With your partner, decide which of these sentences are true based on what you heard. Listen again and check your answers.

1 Shola walked to the area to meet Anastasia.

2 The flat is on a main road.

3 The area has changed over recent years.

4 The weather is sunny and warm on the day they meet.

5 The building where the flat is is old.

6 Anastasia's been looking for a tenant for a while.

7 Anastasia suggests they can share the cooking.

8 Shola really likes rap music.

GRAMMAR

Comparing now and the past

We often make comparisons between situations and things as they are now and as they were in the past.

*There are **a lot more bars** and restaurants **than there used to be**.*

8 Look at these sentences from the conversation. Then work in pairs and answer the questions.

a *There are fewer cars on the road than before.*

b *There's much less crime now.*

c *It's more popular than it used to be.*

d *I'm much thinner than I was.*

e *It was so much worse in the past.*

f *I'm not as fit as I used to be.*

1 Which sentences use nouns in the comparisons? Which use adjectives?

2 When do you use *fewer* to compare and when do you use *less*?

3 What time words and phrases are used to refer to the past?

4 What usually comes first in the sentence – the situation now or the situation in the past?

5 What do you remember about the rules for comparative adjectives from Unit 6?

G Check your ideas on page 86 and do Exercise 1.

9 Work in groups. Discuss the questions.

- What's better and what's worse about your area now compared with the past?
- What's better and what's worse about the city or region you live in?
- What's better and what's worse about your country now?
- What's better and what's worse about your life compared with five years ago?
- What's better and what's worse about the world than it was twenty years ago?

G For further practice, see Exercise 2 on page 87.

DEVELOPING CONVERSATIONS

Asking about rules

In the conversation, you heard Shola check the rules of the house. For example:

S: *Is it OK if I cook here whenever I like?*

A: *Sure – as long as I'm not preparing something.*

When we reply, we often say 'no' using *I'm afraid not* or we suggest limits using *as long as*, *it depends* or *within reason*.

10 Match the questions (1–6) with the replies (a–f). Notice the phrases in bold.

1 **Would it be OK if** I have friends to visit?

2 **Would you mind if** I cooked for myself sometimes?

3 **Do I have to** be home before a certain time?

4 **Can I** use the washing machine whenever I like?

5 **Would it be possible to** move a table into my room?

6 **Is it OK if** I play music in my room?

a **No, not at all – as long as** you're quiet if you're back late.

b **I'm afraid not**, no. The two we have are needed downstairs.

c **Not at all – as long as** you clean up after yourself.

d **It depends how long for**. It's fine if it's just a few days.

e **Of course, within reason**. Obviously, you shouldn't play it too loud.

f **Within reason**. Obviously, I don't want you washing clothes in the middle of the night!

PRONUNCIATION

11 ▶ **44** Listen to the exchanges from Exercise 10 and check your answers. Notice how some words are linked together.

12 Work in pairs. Practise saying the exchanges slowly and concentrate on linking the words. Then practise saying them as quickly as you can.

13 With your partner, roleplay a phone call between a student and a host family. Use as much new language from this unit as you can. When you have finished, change roles and have another conversation.

Student A: you are the student. Ask questions about:
- the house.
- the area.
- rules.
- any special requests.

Student B: you are a member of the host family.

GOING OUT

IN THIS UNIT YOU LEARN HOW TO:

- talk about exhibitions, films and the theatre
- explain exactly where places are
- discuss nights out
- use idioms connected to different parts of the body
- describe different kinds of events
- talk about plans that failed to happen and explain why

SPEAKING

1   Work in pairs. Discuss the questions.

- Do you like the art in this photo? Why? / Why not?
- What point do you think the artist is trying to make with this piece?
- How often do you go to art exhibitions / the cinema / the theatre?
- What kind of art / films / theatre do you like?
- Are there any exhibitions / plays on at the moment that you would like to see?

2   Work with a new partner. Can you think of an example of each of the different kinds of people below? Do you have any favourites?

a painter	a sculptor
a director	a DJ
a stand-up comedian	a singer-songwriter

WHAT'S ON?

VOCABULARY Exhibitions, films and theatre

1 Work in pairs. Decide what the words in each of the groups below have in common.

1 a thriller / a classic / a documentary / a comedy

2 a musical / a tragedy / a historical play / a drama

3 an installation / a landscape / a portrait / a sculpture

4 soundtrack / special effects / photography / plot

5 acting / costumes / lighting / staging

2 With your partner, give examples of as many of the things in Exercise 1 as you can.

A: *One of my favourite thrillers is 'Shutter Island'. Do you know it?*

B: *No, I don't think so. Who's it by?*

A: *Martin Scorsese. It came out maybe five or six years ago.*

3 Match each question (1–6) with two possible answers (a–l).

1 What's on in town at the moment?

2 What kind of exhibition is it?

3 What's it about?

4 When's it on?

5 Who's in it?

6 What was it like?

a They've got showings at 6.00, 8.50 and 11.00.

b Johnny Depp and Morgan Freeman.

c It's a drama about life in a rural community.

d Not much, really. There's a musical on at the theatre that might be OK.

e It's a collection of historical objects from Central America.

f It's on till next week and the gallery's open between 10.00am and 8.00pm.

g It was great. The staging and the lighting were amazing.

h Nobody I've heard of.

i I think it's some kind of romantic comedy.

j There's the new film by that Swedish director Lukas Moodysson.

k It's a series of installations by a Danish artist called Jeppe Hein.

l It was brilliant. The special effects were amazing.

4 Work in pairs. Think of one more possible answer for each of the questions in Exercise 3.

LISTENING

5 ▶ 45 Listen to the first part of a conversation between two friends, Dan and Jason. Answer the questions.

1 What's on?

2 What's it about?

3 When's it on?

4 Where's it on?

6 ▶ **46** Listen to the rest of the conversation. Answer the questions.

1 Where is the cinema? Mark it on the map below.

2 What time do they arrange to meet? Why?

DEVELOPING CONVERSATIONS

Explaining where places are

When explaining where places are, we often start by mentioning places that we think will be known and give directions from there. For example, in the conversation you heard:

You know Oxford Road, yeah? Well, that's the main street which goes past the railway station. Well, if you have your back to the station, you turn right down Oxford Road.

7 Complete the sentences with the words in the boxes.

front	off	next	at	halfway

1 You know Columbus Avenue? Well, the restaurant's about _____ down there.

2 The bus stop is right in _____ of the main entrance to the station.

3 You know the post office? Well, St Ann's Road is the _____ turning down from there, on the other side of the road.

4 You know the cinema? Well, there's a car park _____ the back.

5 You know the main square? Well, Hope Close is one of the streets _____ there.

coming	back	towards	out	facing

6 If you have your _____ to the station, you turn left.

7 If you're _____ the station, the shop will be on your right.

8 If you're _____ down the road away from the station, Church Street's the second turning on the left.

9 If you're going up the road _____ the station and away from the river, Pemberton Road's the second on the right.

10 When you come _____ of the building, you'll see the cinema right opposite.

PRONUNCIATION

8 ▶ **47** Listen to the sentences from Exercise 7 and check your answers.

9 ▶ **47** Listen again. Notice the pauses at the punctuation marks. Practise saying the sentences in the same way.

10 Work in pairs. Take turns to draw small maps to illustrate each of the ten descriptions in Exercise 7. As you draw, explain what your map shows. How good are your partner's drawings?

11 Think of three places near where you live or study that you can describe using language from Exercise 7. Then work in groups and describe where these places are. Can the rest of your group guess the places you mean?

CONVERSATION PRACTICE

12 Work in pairs. Think of a film / exhibition / play you want to invite other students to tonight. It can be a real event or you can invent details. Decide what it is, why you think it'll be good and where and when it's on.

13 Work with a new partner. Have conversations similar to the one you heard in the listening. Take turns being A and B. Use the guide below to help you.

Student A	Student B
Ask Student B if they fancy going out tonight.	
	Ask what's on.
Explain and say why you think it'll be good.	
	Ask some other questions.
Answer. Suggest where / when to meet.	
	Agree to go. Ask where it is exactly. Don't accept the first meeting time that A suggests.

🎥 18 To watch the video and do the activities, see the DVD ROM.

BIG NIGHT OUT

READING

1 Work in groups. You are going to read an article about typical nights out around the world. First, discuss the questions.

- Which day of the week is the main night out for you?
- What do you normally do?
- What time do you go out and get back home?
- How expensive is going out where you live?
- What do you know about the places in the photos? What do you think the nightlife might be like?

2 Now read the article. With the same group, discuss your answers to these questions.

- Which night out sounds most like where you live?
- Which night out sounds the best to you? Why?
- Which sounds the worst? Why?

3 Match the sentences below to the people and places in the article.

- a The nightlife is restricted by the government.
- b They go out into the countryside.
- c Their night out often finishes early.
- d People sometimes get away with breaking the law.
- e They don't like the wealth gap.
- f They think carefully about what they wear.
- g They have been given some useful suggestions.
- h They have changed a habit.

4 Work in pairs. Discuss the questions.

- Do you think you are past anything? Why?
- What restrictions are there on nightlife where you are? Do you agree with them?
- Do you ever go to sports events?
- How do you like to dress when you go out at night?

A Friday night out here in the summer is quite special, as the sun never sets. I usually start with a light meal – **a little** sushi or something like that – and then around midnight, I'll go and play eighteen holes of golf. I'm normally back around four a.m. Saturday I sleep in till the afternoon and have an early dinner – some puffin or whale. I usually go for a swim in one of the natural hot springs till midnight. It depends on my mood what I do next, but these days I'm a bit past clubbing, so I tend to go for a walk and just enjoy our amazing landscape instead.

1 HERDIS Akureyri, Iceland

Thursday is the big night out in Tehran. **Many** students like me start the evening by going for a coffee or maybe sharing a hookah pipe. By twelve, the streets are dead, though. The law says that **no** shops, cafés or restaurants are allowed to open past midnight, but don't be fooled by the silent streets – the city's heart is still beating! We have a saying that what happens behind a closed door is no-one's business, so a lot of people have parties at home and generally the police won't disturb you. There are also **a few** places like Super Jordan where the police turn a blind eye and you can buy supplies after twelve.

2 ANOUSHA Tehran, Iran

3 LINDA Busan, South Korea

During the summer months, a Friday or Saturday night out will normally mean a trip to see the Lotte Giants baseball team. Before I came here, I'd had **little** interest in any sport, but one trip to a game here was enough to convert me to baseball. I go to **every** game now. The atmosphere is incredible. From start to finish, **most** people are cheering and singing the team song, even when the team is getting beaten badly. There's dancing, food, drink, good company – everything you need for a good night out. It usually finishes around nine, but by then I'm exhausted and head home rather than going on somewhere else.

I came to Luanda to teach English. Since the discovery of oil, the economy has boomed and attracted a large foreign community. When I first came here we used to go to restaurants along the bay and they cost an arm and a leg! Even a simple burger is upwards of $20. It's pretty shocking when so **few** local people could afford it and there is still so **much** poverty. Recently, I started doing some volunteer work in a school. Through my colleagues I've been introduced to some places where locals eat, which are miles cheaper. Afterwards, we might go on to a party in someone's backyard and dance till the early hours.

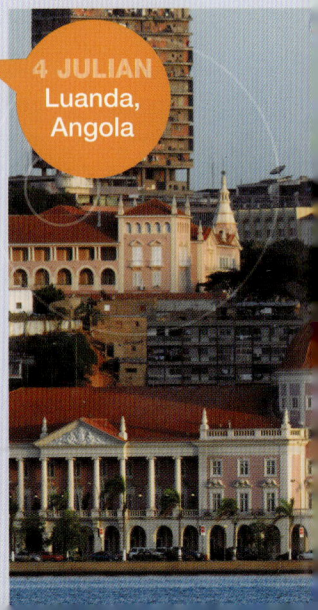

4 JULIAN Luanda, Angola

GRAMMAR

Quantifiers

Quantifiers are words that go before nouns, for example *no chance*, *a lot of places*, *few people*, etc. We use quantifiers to show the quantity of the noun we are talking about.

5 Work in pairs. Match the quantifiers in bold in the article with the basic meanings below.

1 not any _____ NO
2 almost no _____ A FEW , LITTLE
3 some _____ A LITTLE , FEW
4 a lot of _____ MUCH , MANY
5 almost all _____ MOST
6 all _____ EVERY

6 With your partner, explain the difference in use between the following:

1 *a few* and *a little*   3 *much* and *many*
2 *a few* and *few*   4 *no* and *not*

G Check your ideas on page 87 and do Exercise 1.

7 Decide which of the sentences below are true for where you live now. Rewrite the other sentences using different quantifiers to make them true. Then work in groups and compare your ideas.

A lot of people go out on Friday night, but I think most people usually go out on Saturday. Of course, some people go out both nights!

1 Friday is the night that most people go out at night. *MANY* *BUT MOST GO OUT ON SATURDAY*
2 There's very little entertainment at night round here.
3 There are a lot of good clubs near here.
4 Not many people are interested in cinema here.
5 There are a few good restaurants here.
6 Not many parents go out on their own once they've had kids.
7 There are no buses at night so most people drive.
8 Women don't get much hassle when they go out at night here.

G For further practice, see Exercise 2 on page 87.

UNDERSTANDING VOCABULARY

Idioms

An idiom is a fixed group of words that mean something different to the meaning of the individual words. You can sometimes work out the meaning of an idiom from the words and the context. If you look up the idiom in a dictionary, it's usually listed under the entry for the noun.

In the article, you read *It cost me an arm and a leg* and *The police often turn a blind eye*. We often use parts of the body in idioms.

8 Complete the definitions with these parts of the body. You will need to use some of the words more than once.

arm	back	eye	face	feet	hand	leg

1 If you **turn a blind** EYE _____ , you know people might be doing something wrong, but you ignore it.
2 If something **costs an** _____ **and a leg**, it is very expensive.
3 If you **give someone a** _____ , you help them.
4 If you **are on your** _____ for a long time, you are standing. Afterwards, you will probably want to **put your** _____ **up** – sit or lie down and relax.
5 If you **try to catch someone's** _____ , you try to get their attention.
6 If you **can't take your** _____ **s off** someone or something happening, you keep looking because the person or thing is so attractive or interesting.
7 If you talk or do something **behind someone's** _____ , you say or do something unkind when the person doesn't realise what you're doing.
8 If you **make** or **pull a** _____ , your expression shows you don't like something.
9 If you say '**I'm just pulling your** _____ ', it means that you are not being serious, you're just joking.
10 If a situation or argument **gets out of** _____ , it becomes a problem that is difficult to control.

9 Work in pairs. Think of a night out you might have. Give examples of when you could use the idioms in bold in Exercise 8.

When I go to a restaurant, I try to catch the waiter's eye to ask for the bill.

Thursday nights I occasionally go and see a stand-up comedy show, but at the weekend I mainly go clubbing as I love dancing. Because of the way I am and the way I want to live, I dress in a certain way, which sometimes attracts people's attention. But I'm not going to change – as Oscar Wilde said, you can never be overdressed or overeducated! The only things I don't wear are high heel shoes. I can't dance like I want to in them, and if you're out all night your feet hurt too much by the time you get home!

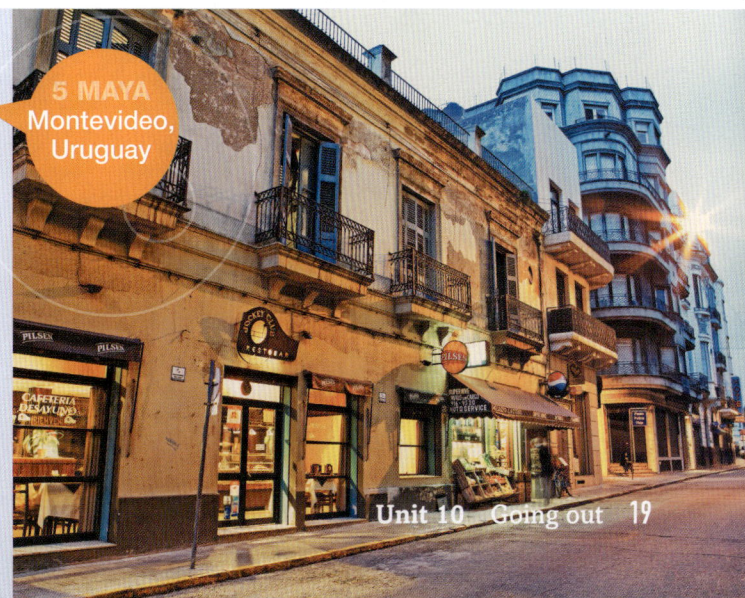

5 MAYA
Montevideo, Uruguay

A CHANGE OF PLAN

SPEAKING

1 Write down three places you have been to in the evening recently and think about the following:

- where each place is
- who you went with
- how often you go there
- what it was like

Now work in groups. Talk about your places and ask each other questions to find out more.

VOCABULARY Describing events

2 Match the sentences (1–8) with the follow-up comments (a–h).

1 It was a great exhibition, but the paintings were quite **weird**.
2 It's not a bad film, but I thought it was a bit **overrated**.
3 It was really **moving**.
4 **It was completely sold out**.
5 It attracts a much older crowd.
6 The **headline band** were rubbish – just very dull.
7 It was **boiling hot** in there.
8 It was an **amazing** night. There was **such a great atmosphere**.

a Honestly, we were really sweating and we could hardly breathe.
b I can't really describe them or say why I like them.
c It **wasn't as great as** everyone's been saying.
d It was **absolutely packed** in there.
e I was **in tears** by the end.
f The music, the audience, everything.
g I **felt a bit out of place**, actually.
h We actually **left halfway through**.

3 Work in pairs. What are the opposites of the words and phrases in bold in Exercise 2?

4 Work in groups. Think of examples of the following:

1 two artists / musicians / films that you think are quite weird
2 two famous films / sports stars that you agree are overrated
3 two films / TV shows / news events that you found really moving
4 two situations when you might feel a bit out of place
5 two other things you could leave halfway through, apart from a concert

LISTENING

5 ▶ **48** Listen to three conversations about what people did last night. Answer the questions about each of the conversations.

1 What kind of event was it?
2 Did they change their plans? If so, why?
3 Did they have a good night? Why? / Why not?
4 Did their experiences match what other people had said about the event they went to?

WAN CHENG REN

6 ▶ **48** Listen again and complete the sentences with three words in each space. Contractions count as one word.

1 a Really? I'd heard it _____ .
  b Maybe it's because I didn't think it'd _____ .
  c And then you go and you just end up thinking it was _____ .

2 a Oh, we didn't go _____ .
  b Well, that's _____ really good. It's quite trendy, isn't it?
  c Oh dear. Maybe you just went on _____ .

3 a I thought you said you were going to have a _____ .
  b She mentioned she had _____ for this play in town.
  c It's had _____ in the papers.

7 Work in pairs. Discuss the questions.

- Who do you think had the best night? Why?
- Can you think of any recent films that had a lot of advance publicity?
- Do you ever go to concerts? If yes, what was the last one you went to? Was it any good?
- Can you think of anything that's had great reviews in the papers recently?

GRAMMAR

The future in the past

There are several different ways of talking about plans, promises or predictions made in the past. Often the reason these things are mentioned is because they then failed to happen or to come true.

8 Look at these sentences from the conversations. Answer the questions below.

a *Hans **was going to pick** me **up** at seven.*
b *I **was going to stay** in.*
c *It was brilliant – much better than I thought it**'d be**.*
d *I didn't think it**'d be** anything special.*
e *I said I**'d go** with her.*

1 In sentences a) and b), did the plans actually happen? Why? / Why not?
2 What structure is used in sentences a) and b)?
3 What were the original thoughts / promises that sentences c), d) and e) are describing?
4 What is *'d* short for in sentences c), d) and e)?
5 What tense is used in sentences c), d) and e)?

Ⓖ Check your ideas on page 88 and do Exercise 1.

9 Make sentences using the prompts below. Link the ideas using *but* and *so*.

I / go out / feel exhausted / just stay in and go to bed early

I was going to go out, but I felt exhausted so I just stayed in and went to bed early.

1 They / have a barbecue / start pouring with rain / have to cook indoors instead
2 We / go to the beach for the day / miss the train / end up going to the park instead
3 She / give me a lift / car not start / get a taxi instead
4 I / walk here / start pouring with rain / have to drive
5 I / stay in and study / a friend call me / go out / meet him

10 Work in pairs. Think of as many different endings for each sentence as you can.

1 We were going to stay with friends, but …
2 I was going to stay in last night, but in the end …
3 She said she was going to call me, but …
4 I was going to buy a new one, but in the end …
5 I really thought we were going to crash, but …

11 Work in groups and discuss the questions. Use the future in the past to explain your ideas.

- Can you think of a time you had a last-minute change of plan? What happened? Did it turn out well / badly?
- Have you ever been very disappointed or pleasantly surprised by a film, party etc. you went to? Why?
- Can you think of any predictions that have failed to come true?
- Have your parents ever promised to do something and then not done it? How did you feel about it?
- Has the government / local council in your country broken any of its promises? What did they say they would do?
- Have you ever broken a promise? What happened?

Ⓖ For further practice, see Exercise 2 on page 88.

VIDEO 5

ONE WOMAN'S CHOICE

1 **Work in pairs. Discuss the questions.**

- Where do you think this photo was taken?
- What do you think life there is like? What problems might people have?
- Why might people from an area like this move to a city?
- Why might people from a city move to live there?

2 📹 **19** **Watch the first part of the video about a woman, Flora, who lives near where the photo was taken (0.00–2.32). Are the sentences true (T) or false (F)?**

1 Flora grew up in the city.
2 Flora is uneducated.
3 She had an arranged marriage.
4 The village they live in has no electricity or water.
5 Most of the Dorobo people raise cattle and farm crops.
6 Her husband is often away from home.
7 Flora regularly sees her own parents and family.
8 She sometimes regrets the decisions she has made.

3 **Work in groups. Discuss what you think of Flora and her situation and what you think she will do.**

4 📹 **19** **Watch the next part of the video, where Flora visits her mother (2.33–4.24). Answer the questions.**

1 What kind of place is Arusha and why is it important?
2 How do you think Flora feels about the city?
3 When was the last time Flora saw her mother?

4 Did Flora have a good or bad relationship with her mother?
5 What does her mother think she should do?
6 What do *you* think Flora will do?

5 📹 **19** **Watch the final part of the video (4.25–5.20). Find out what Flora decides to do – and the reasons she gives for her decision.**

6 **Work in pairs. Discuss the questions.**

- What do you think of Flora's decision and reasons?
- Could you live where Flora does? Why? / Why not?
- In your country, where would you rather live: in the city or in the country? Why?
- Do you know anyone who has made a big change in their lives? Why? What happened?

UNDERSTANDING FAST SPEECH

7 📹 **20** **Read and listen to this extract from the video said at natural pace and then slowed down. To help you, groups of words are marked with / and pauses are marked //. Stressed sounds are in CAPITALS.**

FLOra's FAMily KNEW / that she was LEAving the COMforts of the CIty // for a WORLD without Electricity / or ALmost ANY / MOdern conVENiences // a WORLD where it TAKES a FORty-MINute WALK / JUST to get WAter

8 **Now you have a go! Practise saying the extract at natural pace.**

REVIEW 5

GRAMMAR

1 Complete the text with one word in each space.

In general, the crime rate [1]_____ fallen quite dramatically [2]_____ recent years. There are [3]_____ robberies than there [4]_____ five years ago and there's [5]_____ violent crime. There were [6]_____ any murders last year. This may well have something to do with the fact that there are [7]_____ policemen on the street than there [8]_____ to be.

However, online crime has [9]_____ increasing steadily over the [10]_____ few years. [11]_____ bank account is completely safe anymore and [12]_____ bank is working hard to improve online security.

2 Choose the correct option.

1 House prices have *increased / been increasing* 50% in the last six months.

2 I have *little / few* interest in politics.

3 *All the / Every* people I work with really love the new boss we've got.

4 It was much better than I thought it *will / would* be.

5 The cost of energy isn't *as / more* low as it used to be.

6 We *are / were* going to go and see a movie, but we didn't in the end.

7 It's not a bad area, but it's not as *well / good* as it used to be.

8 Unemployment *has / has been* fallen steadily over recent years.

9 Would you like a *few / little* more cake?

10 I'm a bit fitter than I *would be / was* this time last year.

3 Complete the second sentence so that it has a similar meaning to the first sentence using the word given. Do not change the word given. You must use between three and five words, including the word given.

1 It's better now than it used to be.
It was _____ than it is now. **PAST**

2 There are fewer jobs available these days.
There _____ jobs available. **BE**

3 I was really surprised by how good it was.
I honestly didn't _____ anything special, but it was amazing. **THINK**

4 They said they don't expect to find any survivors.
They said there's not _____ finding any survivors. **HOPE**

5 I usually do portraits, but I also occasionally do landscapes.
_____ , I do portraits, but I also do some landscapes occasionally. **TIME**

6 Inflation was 5% at the start of the year and now it's almost 18%.
Inflation _____ the start of the year. **DRAMATICALLY**

4 ▶ 49 Listen and write the six sentences you hear.

VOCABULARY

5 Match the verbs (1–8) with the collocates (a–h).

1	feel	a	north
2	rent	b	the waiter's eye
3	face	c	a face
4	catch	d	a blind eye
5	pull	e	halfway through
6	give	f	out of place
7	turn	g	you a hand
8	leave	h	a shared apartment

6 Decide if these words and phrases are connected to houses, the arts or areas.

cramped	an attic	lively	rough
a classic	compact	a patio	staging
a landscape	a plot	well connected	dead

7 Complete the sentences. Use the word in brackets to form a word that fits in the space.

1 We went to see this really funny new stand-up _____ last night. (comedy)

2 It was an interesting _____ . It was a series of _____ that all use mirrors in different ways. (exhibit, install)

3 It was good. It was a _____ play set in the 1930s. (history)

4 It's an amazing play. The acting's wonderful and the _____ is very clever. (light)

5 I'd like to study _____ at art college if I can. (photograph)

6 It's a nice place. It's much more _____ than her old flat. (space)

7 It's not a cheap place to live, but it is quite _____ . (centre)

8 The government has recently changed its position on _____ . (immigrant)

8 Complete the email with one word in each space. The first letters are given.

Hi Ian,

How are you? Hope you're well.

We're all on our last legs here. We've been looking at houses for the last few weeks and it's a very tiring process. We saw a lovely [1]pl_____ yesterday, though. Do you know Church Street? Well, it's in a little street [2]o_____ there, about halfway [3]d_____ on the left. It's only two minutes from the station, so it's [4]co_____ for transport and the area's quite smart as well – not much [5]li_____ on the streets and no [6]gr_____ on the walls or anything. Amazingly, though, the place itself is still quite [7]af_____ . I was expecting everything round there to cost an a[8]_____ and a leg. Anyway, it's very modern – newly-[9]b_____ , I think – and it's lovely and [10]br_____ , with great big windows facing south. There's a [11]ga_____ for the car and a back [12]ga_____ for the kids to play in.

We put an offer in this morning and we're waiting to hear if it's been accepted.

11

THE NATURAL WORLD

IN THIS UNIT YOU LEARN HOW TO:

- tell and participate in telling stories
- describe animals
- show emotions through pronunciation
- talk about challenges and achievements
- discuss natural resources and the economy

SPEAKING

1 **Work in groups. Look at the photo and discuss the questions.**
- Why do you think the prisoners were given dogs?
- Do you think letting prisoners look after dogs is a good idea? Why? / Why not?
- Have you got a pet? If yes, what and why? If not, why not?

2 **Look at the photos in File 16 on page 98 and discuss the questions.**
- Which of these animals do you like? Why?
- Are you scared of any of these animals? Why?
- Would any of them make good pets?

SO WHAT HAPPENED?

VOCABULARY Movements and sounds

1 Work in groups. You have one minute. Which group can write down the most names of animals in English?

2 Work in pairs. Check you understand the words and phrases in bold in the sentences below. Think of two animals for each sentence that the speaker may have seen or heard.

   1 Oh look, what are they? Can you see them **circling in the sky above that cliff**?

   2 What was that? Did you see it? It just **disappeared into the long grass**.

   3 Oh look, what's that **lying on the rock**?

   4 Did you see that? It just **raced across the road**.

   5 Oh, look! What's that thing **crawling along the floor**?

   6 Did you see that? Something **leapt out of the water**.

   7 Can you hear that **noise in the distance**?

   8 What's making that **dreadful noise**? Are they birds?

   9 Can you hear that? There's something **moving around in the bushes**.

   10 Oh, what's that **buzzing noise**? It's really irritating.

3 Tell your partner about six animals you have seen in the wild or in your town. Try to use language from Exercise 2.

   When I went to Spain last year, I saw some vultures circling above our campsite.

   The other day, I saw a rat crawling along the railway tracks.

LISTENING

4 ▶ 50 Listen to three stories about animals. Answer the questions.

   1 What animal(s) is each story about?

   2 Where were the speakers at the time? What were they doing?

   3 How did each speaker feel?

5 ▶ 50 Work in pairs. Decide in which story you heard the following. Explain how you think each sentence is connected to the story. Then listen again and check your ideas.

   a I really thought they were going to eat me.

   b I managed to catch it and put it into a box.

   c They were all making this dreadful noise.

   d It's so cute!

   e It must've escaped from somewhere.

   f She crawled through a little hole.

   g Honestly, I hope I never see another crocodile in my life!

   h We had to call the fire service in the end.

   i Everyone ran away.

PRONUNCIATION

6 ▶ 51 Listen to eight sentences. Notice the extra stress and long vowel sound on the adverbs. They help to emphasise how we feel. Then listen again and repeat.

7 Underline the adverbs below that you think could carry an extra stress. Then work in pairs. Take turns to say the paragraph. Whose version sounds best?

I don't really like dogs, but I really hate some dog owners. They can be so annoying – the way they talk about their pets like they were actually human beings! They say things like, 'Oh, my little baby. You're so beautiful! Yes, you are. Yes, you are.' It's so stupid. What really annoys me, though, is the way they let their dogs run out of control. They even let their dogs jump on top of you. Then, if the dog bites you, they actually blame you. They say you scared the dog!

GRAMMAR

Past ability / obligation

We use *could* with sense verbs like *see*, *hear*, *feel*, etc.

We use *couldn't* to talk about inability or a specific failure.

We use *managed to* to show an ability to do something difficult at a particular time.

We use *had to* for past obligations or for when there was no choice.

8 Work in pairs. Look at the mistakes crossed out in these sentences. Decide what the correct form should be according to the Grammar box.

1 I ~~must~~ put some fruit and seeds on the ground to tempt it down and when it came down I ~~can~~ catch it and put it into a box.

2 We ~~can~~ hear these little cries coming from somewhere, but we ~~can't~~ see her anywhere.

3 We ~~must~~ call the fire service in the end, and they ~~can~~ get her out.

Ⓖ Check your ideas on page 88 and do Exercise 1.

9 Work in pairs. Choose four of the situations below. Write two sentences for each situation using *had to*, *managed to*, *could* or *couldn't* that might explain what happened and / or how you resolved the situation.

1 Your cat got stuck in a tree.

2 You were driving in the countryside and hit a sheep.

3 You fell and hurt yourself when walking in the mountains.

4 Your bag was stolen just before you travelled home from holiday.

5 You locked yourself out of your second-floor flat.

DEVELOPING CONVERSATIONS

Helping people to tell stories

Good listeners ask questions when people tell stories. For example, in the listening you heard:

F: *I really thought they were going to eat me.*

E: *Really? That sounds terrifying!* **So what happened?**

F: *Well, luckily, the guides managed to stop the lizards.*

10 Complete the conversations with these questions.

What was that doing there?	Seriously?
What was that?	What?
So what happened in the end?	

1 A: You'll never guess what happened last night.
  B: Go on. ¹_____
  A: Well, I was walking home when I suddenly saw a horse standing there in the street!

2 C: I saw something really strange while we were away.
  D: Oh yeah? ²_____
  C: We saw this whale stuck on the beach.
  D: ³_____ Still alive?
  C: Yeah! It was actually quite upsetting! We phoned the police to see if they could organise help.

3 E: I was just about to put my shoes on when I found a scorpion hiding in one of the shoes!
  F: Really? ⁴_____
  E: I don't know. I guess it was just looking for somewhere to sleep.

4 G: We spent hours trying to persuade the cat to come down from the tree, but it refused to come.
  H: Oh no. That's awful! ⁵_____
  G: Well, eventually, we gave up, but an hour later it walked into the kitchen, looking for its dinner!

11 ▶ 52 Listen and check your answers. Then work in pairs and practise reading aloud the conversations.

CONVERSATION PRACTICE

12 Work with a new partner. Each choose one of these ideas for a story and spend a few minutes making notes. Then tell each other your stories, starting with *Did I tell you what happened …?* Help your partner by making comments and asking questions as in Exercise 10.

- a story about your pet
- a story about a time you saw a wild animal
- a story based on the ideas in Exercise 10

🎥 21 To watch the video and do the activities, see the DVD ROM.

CHALLENGES AND ACHIEVEMENTS

SPEAKING

1 Work in groups. Discuss the questions.

- Do you spend much time in nature? Where do you go?

- Have you been to one of these places? When? Where? What was it like?
  - a desert
  - a glacier
  - the summit of a mountain
  - the middle of the ocean

- Do you know any stories of people doing the following challenges? Were they successful? Why? / Why not?
  - sailing round the world
  - reaching the North Pole
  - crossing a desert
  - jumping from a high altitude

READING

2 Work in pairs. You are going to read an article. First, look at the main photo opposite and discuss the questions.

1 Where is it?

2 What's happening?

3 What might be the problem?

3 Read the first three paragraphs of the article and answer the questions in Exercise 2.

4 Work in groups. Choose six words from the box and discuss how you think they will relate to Wilson's story. Then read the rest of the article and find out what happened.

barriers	solo	tent
shot	achievement	blind
partially	disguise	supplies
authorities	expedition	desperately
territory	storm	optimism

5 Work with the same group. Discuss the questions, based on your knowledge of the world, what you understand from the text and your opinions.

1 Why do you think he was refused entry into Tibet and Nepal?

2 Why do you think flying solo to India was described as 'a huge achievement'?

3 Why do you think he ignored the climbing equipment?

4 Why do you think he was starving, half blind and in great pain?

5 What do you think happened to the Sherpas?

6 What do you think drove Wilson to do what he did?

7 In what ways do you think Wilson is the same or different to the amateurs talked about at the beginning of the article?

8 What do you think of Wilson?

LISTENING

6 ▶ 53 Listen to someone talking about the article you read. How does he answer questions 6, 7 and 8 in Exercise 5? Do you agree with the speaker? Why? / Why not?

VOCABULARY Challenges and achievements

7 Complete the sentences below with these pairs of words and phrases.

set myself a target + achieve
overcome many barriers + disabled
scared + overcame my fear
peak + reached the summit
ambition + reaching my goal
tough + get through the pain
took several attempts + determination
dreamt + my dream's come true

1 I climbed the highest _____ in Europe – Mont Blanc. I was so happy when I _____ , I can't express it.

2 A year ago I did the Marathon des Sables challenge, which is a 254km race through the Sahara desert. It was very _____ , but I managed to _____ and finish.

3 Until last year, I'd never been in the sea because I was so _____ of drowning, but last year I had some swimming lessons and I finally _____ . I was so proud of myself!

4 My biggest ever challenge was giving up smoking. It _____ and a lot of strength and _____ , but I finally managed to do it. My son is very proud of me!

5 I've always _____ of becoming a writer and now _____ because my book is going to be published.

6 My _____ is to become a millionaire before I'm 40 and I'm well on the way to _____ .

7 I _____ of learning 50 words or phrases each week. I'm sure I can _____ it.

8 I'm blind so I think getting a degree and a good job has been a big achievement as you have to _____ when you're _____ .

8 Work in groups. Discuss the questions.

- What do you think is the biggest challenge / achievement in Exercise 7?

- What examples can you think of of successful people who have overcome a barrier or disability?

- Do you set yourself any targets for learning English? Do you achieve them?

- What are your three biggest achievements so far?

- What dreams or ambitions do you have? How close are you to making them come true?

THE STRANGE STORY OF
MAURICE WILSON

Looking at the photo – the clear blue sky and queues of people – you might think that this is a group of walkers on a summer's day climbing a popular local peak. But this is the summit of Everest – almost 9,000 metres high, with temperatures of -15 and winds blowing at 50km/h on a 'good' day. What's more, at this altitude the lack of oxygen can cause confusion, slow your movements and make it almost impossible to keep warm. It's so dangerous they call this place 'the Death Zone'.

Some argue that pictures like this create a false impression. They attract too many amateurs who have a romantic idea of reaching 'the top of the world' and are rich enough to pay $70,000 to make their dream come true. However, they have no proper concept of the risks when they climb Everest. They rely too heavily on using fixed ropes and the support of their guides and they don't have the skill or experience to cope when things go wrong.

Maurice Wilson

But amateurs on Everest are nothing new. In the 1930s, some eighty years before this photo was taken, a man called Maurice Wilson attempted to climb Everest. His plan was to fly from Britain and land on the Great Rongbuk glacier, and from there go to the top. There were only two problems – he didn't know how to fly a plane and he'd never climbed before.

In fact these weren't the only barriers to achieving his goal. He had been shot during the First World War and could only partially use his left arm. The British government tried to stop him even getting to India because they saw him as dangerous; the authorities in Nepal and Tibet also refused to let him enter their territory.

Incredibly, then, just two months after his first flying lesson, he managed to fly solo all the way to India in a tiny second-hand plane – a huge achievement for the time.

He then managed to enter Tibet by disguising himself as a Tibetan monk and walked several hundred miles to reach the Rongbuk monastery at the foot of Everest.

Without a guide, Wilson set off up the glacier. He frequently got lost among the towers of ice and it took him three days to reach Camp 2, which had been established by a previous expedition. There was climbing equipment at the camp but he ignored it and continued up the mountain. At 6,500 metres a storm hit and he was forced to sit in his tent for two and a half days. When the storm eased he struggled back to the monastery – starving, half blind and his arm in great pain.

However, he rested for just two days before he tried again. This time he persuaded two local Sherpas to help him carry supplies up the mountain and guide him through the glacier. With their help he went higher up to Camp 3 but once again high winds and snow stopped them going further. As the weather cleared, Wilson continued up the mountain on his own, reaching around 7,500 metres before returning to Camp 3. He was by this time exhausted and six days at such high altitude was giving him headaches. The Sherpas desperately tried to persuade him to give up, but Wilson insisted on trying one more time. The last words in his diary are still full of optimism. 'Off again. Gorgeous day.' He never returned. His body was found a year later. He was wearing green boots, a grey suit and a purple jersey – almost as if ready for a walk in the park on a chilly London afternoon.

GLOSSARY

a monk = a member of a group of religious men who live away from other people
a monastery = a religious place where monks live and pray
a Sherpa = a mountain person in Tibet and Nepal

NATURAL RESOURCES

READING

1 **Work in pairs. Discuss the questions.**

1 Do you know which country has the most natural resources (oil, coal, gas, etc.)?

2 Which countries do you think produce the most oil and coal?

3 Where do you think the biggest oil companies are from?

4 How long do you think the coal, oil and gas that we still have will last?

5 Do you think countries rich in natural resources are wealthier than those without?

2 **Read the fact file. Find the answers to the questions in Exercise 1.**

3 **Match the words in bold in the fact file to the meanings below.**

1 use a resource or product

2 take something out of somewhere, often with difficulty

3 areas of a country where they take oil from the ground

4 the speed at which something is happening at the moment

5 the available amount or supply of something that a country has

6 make a hole (usually round) with a tool or machine

7 something causing disagreement or anger among the public

8 dig a big hole or tunnel in the ground to get gold etc.

4 **Work in groups. Do you find each fact in the fact file surprising, unsurprising, interesting or depressing? Explain why.**

FACT FILE

Russia is the richest country in terms of natural resources. It has the biggest **reserves** of natural gas and wood. In addition, it has the world's second-largest reserves of coal and the third-largest reserves of gold. However, in terms of average wealth per person, it's not even in the top 50 countries.

Nigeria is the largest producer of oil in Africa. It is one of the 20 poorest countries in the world. Many people who live in its **oil-producing regions** earn less than $1 a day.

India is the third biggest coal producer. In terms of average wealth per person, India comes 130th in the world.

China is the world's biggest producer of coal. It **mines** over 47% of the world's total.

The USA is the biggest oil producer in the world, bigger than Saudi Arabia. There's been some **controversy** about how it **drills** for oil in the sea.

Only three of the 25 biggest oil companies in the world are American. The three biggest are Saudi, Russian and Iranian.

If we **consume** coal at **the current rate** it will last for two hundred years. Some argue oil will run out in 50 years and gas will run out in 60 years. Others say there is more than that, but it's very expensive to **extract** from the ground.

LISTENING

5 ▶ 54 You are going to hear the introduction of a short talk on 'the resource curse'. What do you think it is? Listen and find out.

6 ▶ 54 Listen to the introduction again and complete these notes.

'Resource curse' – 1990's – by ¹_____ Auty

People in resource-rich countries ²_____ than others

Four reasons: conflict, corruption, value of manufactured products, ³_____

Conflict

Local people ⁴_____ leave land. No compensation

⁵_____ want independence ➡ civil war

Corruption

Companies pay officials to avoid ⁶_____

Manufacturing

Manufactured goods like ⁷_____ more ⁸_____

If you have no resources ➡ manufacturing ➡ economy ⁹_____

Why not invest?

Economic ¹⁰_____ ➡ reduced investment

Prices vary:

◆ fall ➡ crisis

◆ rise ➡ currency rises ➡ imports ¹¹_____ ,
exporting ¹²_____ ➡ factories can't sell ➡ less investment

---

7 Work in pairs. Discuss the questions.

- Had you heard of 'the resource curse' before?
- Do you think it is always true? Can you think of any examples where it is different?
- Have you any idea how it might be avoided?

8 ▶ 55 Listen to a later part of the talk about a country that has a natural resource. Find out:

1 which country it is.
2 what was discovered.
3 what happened to the money.
4 what made this possible.

GRAMMAR

Passives

We make passives using a form of the verb *be* + past participle.

We usually use passives when:

1 we want to focus on the person / thing affected by an action – rather than on the doer of an action.

2 we don't know who or what did an action.

3 when it's simply not important – or it's obvious – who did an action.

---

9 Look at these sentences from the talk. Answer the questions below.

a *This phrase **was** first **used** in the 1990s by the writer Richard Auty.*

b *Local people **are** often **forced** to leave their land …*

c *… so that resources **can be extracted** …*

d *For over 40 years now, profits **have been invested** in health care …*

1 What tenses are used in sentences a), b) and d)?
2 What passive form follows modal verbs?
3 Which sentence gives the person / thing doing the action? Which word is used to introduce the doer?
4 Who or what do you think did the actions in the other sentences?

G Check your ideas on page 89 and do Exercise 1.

10 Complete the sentences with the correct passive form of the verbs.

1 Most of their gas and oil _____ from abroad. (import)

2 The city grew a lot after gold _____ near there. (discover)

3 Wind farms _____ over the country at the moment. (construct)

4 Solar energy is cheap here because it _____ by the government. (subsidise)

5 Locals don't want the drilling to take place because they believe their houses _____ . (damage)

6 More could _____ to exploit our resources, but the government often faces protests. (do)

7 A lot of money _____ from our natural resources but it _____ wisely. (make, not / invest)

11 Work in groups. Use the sentences in Exercise 10 to talk about places you know.

Most of the gas in our country is imported from abroad. It mainly comes from Russia.

I think Dubai only grew after oil was discovered there.

G For further practice, see Exercise 2 on page 89.

SPEAKING

12 Imagine a natural resource was suddenly discovered in your country. What should the money be spent on? Rank the ideas below from 1 (= most important) to 7 (= least important).

- building more airports and motorways
- providing free university-level education for everyone
- building factories that can process the raw material
- giving $10,000 to every family
- bringing as many women into the workplace as possible
- improving health care
- increasing wages of people enforcing laws (police, tax inspectors, judges, etc.)

13 Work in groups. Compare your lists then try to agree on the best two ways to spend the money.

IN THIS UNIT YOU LEARN HOW TO:

- describe character
- talk about your friends and family
- explain how people you know are similar
- talk about memories
- express regrets
- talk about relationships

SPEAKING

1 **Work in pairs. Discuss the questions.**

- What do you think the relationship is between the different people in the photo?
- What are the advantages and disadvantages of living with your extended family?
- Who are the oldest and youngest people in your family?

2 **Talk to other students and find who:**

1 lives with more than one generation of their family.
2 has the most brothers and sisters.
3 has the most nephews and nieces.
4 has the oldest relative.
5 has a half-brother or half-sister.
6 has a step-brother or step-sister.
7 has family members living in another country.

3 **Work with your partner again and compare what you found out. What was the most interesting thing you learned?**

PEOPLE I KNOW

FAMILY AND FRIENDS

VOCABULARY Describing character

1 **Complete the sentences below with the words in the boxes.**

| creative | intense | loyal | sensitive | bright | calm |

1 He's a great friend to have. He's very _____ – always there for you when you need him.

2 She's very _____ . I mean, she draws, she paints, she plays the guitar.

3 He's one of the smartest guys I know – just very clever, very _____ .

4 She's always very _____ and relaxed, even when everyone else is stressing about things.

5 He's very _____ . I mean, he gets upset very easily and he takes things very personally.

6 Some people find her quite hard to get on with because she's so focused, so _____ .

| ambitious | charming | competitive | direct |
| diplomatic | modest | | |

7 He's a very _____ man. I mean, he's very popular with the ladies.

8 She's always very _____ . She never upsets anyone or makes anyone angry.

9 She's very _____ . She always says what she means.

10 He's highly _____ . He really pushes himself.

11 He's very successful, but he's also incredibly _____ . He never shows off or anything.

12 She's very sporty and very _____ . She always wants to win and she really hates losing!

PRONUNCIATION

2 **Work in pairs. Say the adjectives in the boxes in Exercise 1 and decide where the main stress is.**

creative

3 ▶ 56 **Listen and check your answers. Then practise saying the adjectives with the correct stress.**

4 **Work in pairs. Discuss the questions.**

1 Can you think of three other things creative people might do?

2 What kind of things might a very charming person often say or do?

3 In what ways is being ambitious a good thing? And in what ways could it be bad?

4 In what ways is being sensitive a bad thing? And in what ways could it be good?

5 Do you like people to be modest about their achievements? Why? / Why not?

6 Do you prefer people to be direct or a bit more diplomatic? Why?

7 Can you think of times when it's good *not* to be very competitive?

8 Can you think of times when it's a bad thing to be very loyal?

5 Work in groups. Tell each other which adjectives you think best describe the people below and explain why.

- other people in your family
- friends of yours
- yourself
- other students in the class

LISTENING

6 ▶ **57** Listen to a man called Lewis talking to his friend, Jessica, about her family. Answer the questions.

1 Why does Lewis start asking about Jessica's brother, Noel?
2 In what way is Lewis's mum similar to Noel?
3 What's Noel like?
4 What does Jessica think of her younger brother?
5 Why is she a bit annoyed at the end of the conversation?

7 ▶ **57** Listen again and complete the sentences with three words in each space. Contractions count as one word.

1 Yeah, sorry. I had to _____ my brother, Noel.
2 I know. I was only _____ five minutes …
3 OK, _____ , but she is very talkative.
4 No, he _____ to study Physics.
5 I don't think _____ before.
6 I don't know. He's just so sensitive. I seem _____ a lot, anyway.
7 You need to be ambitious, _____ , or you'll never make any money.
8 Well, I guess you get _____ in the art world …

8 Work in pairs. Discuss the questions.

- As a child, which is worst: being the oldest, the youngest or in the middle?
- Do you know any brothers or sisters who are very different to each other? In what way?
- Do you know anyone who has won a scholarship? Where to?
- Which of these sentences best describes what you think about Jessica?
  a She's too hard on her brother. She should support him more.
  b It's fine to tell her brother what she thinks, but maybe she should be more diplomatic.
  c She's right to be hard on him. He sounds like he needs a push!
  d She actually sounds quite sensitive herself!

DEVELOPING CONVERSATIONS

That's like …
When people tell us about the character or habits of someone, we often compare the person to someone similar that we know. To introduce our comments, we often use *That's like …*

J: *Once he starts talking, he doesn't stop!*
L: *Oh, **that's like** my mum. She can talk for hours.*

9 Match the sentences (1–6) with the comments (a–f).

1 He never does anything around the house.
2 He's only three and whenever he sees me, he runs up and gives me a big hug. It's so sweet.
3 He's so serious. All he ever talks about is politics. You can never just have a laugh with him.
4 She just lets her son do whatever he wants. She really spoils him.
5 She's very shy. She's not very good with people.
6 She works really hard and she's very focused and ambitious.

a That's like my cousin. He finds it quite hard to make new friends.
b That's like my brother-in-law. He's very intense.
c That's like my brother. He's only 23, but he's already running his own company.
d That's a bit like a friend of mine. He never says 'no' either – and his kid's really naughty.
e That's just like my sister. She's really lazy too.
f Ah! That's like my niece. They're so cute at that age.

10 Work in pairs. Student A: read out sentences 1–6. Student B: say the matching comment, but change the people so the sentences are true for you. Then change roles and repeat.

A: *He never does anything around the house.*
B: *That's just like my brother Dan. He's really lazy.*

CONVERSATION PRACTICE

11 Think of three family members you want to talk about. If you have photos of them on your phone, find them. Decide how to answer the questions below for each person.

- How old is he / she?
- What's he / she like? Do you get on well?
- Are you close? Do you see him / her a lot?
- What does he / she do?
- Where does he / she live? Is it near here?

12 Work in groups. Talk about your family and show photos if you have any. Ask each other the questions above and any others you can think of. Add comparisons with your own friends and family when you can. Use *That's like …*

🎥 22 To watch the video and do the activities, see the DVD ROM.

THE OLDER GENERATION

READING

1 **Work in groups. Discuss the questions.**

- At what age would you describe someone as old?
- Do you think it's better to be an old person or a young person in your country? Why?
- How often do you spend time with people of a different generation?
- Have your grandparents played an important role in your life? Why? / Why not?

2 **Check you understand these words, which are from an article you are going to read. Then work in groups and discuss which words you associate with grandparents. Explain your ideas.**

career	wrinkly	childcare	indulgent
a pipe	active	sacrifice	discipline

Is this how grandmothers still are?

STRUGGLING TO FIT INTO THE ROLE OF GRANNY

Jean Winship is finding it hard to adapt to life as a grandparent – and claims she's not alone.

I am a grandma. I've been trying hard to get used to the idea ever since my daughter gave birth last year, but fourteen months on, I'm still not quite sure how I feel. It doesn't help that my daughter has started referring to me as Granny Jean. Obviously, I'm happy for my daughter and think her son, Ollie, is gorgeous, but *Granny*? [1]_____ I only recently turned 50. I still have a career, big nights out and holidays in unusual countries.

I suspect that one of the reasons I'm not yet comfortable with my new status is that very little about my life matches the vague memories I have of my own grandparents. My dad's parents both died before I was born and the only thing I can really remember about my other grandfather was that he often smoked a pipe. I used to love the smell of the fresh tobacco. [2]_____ After he died, Gran moved to a town by the seaside and we'd go and visit for a week each summer. I have fond memories of her because she'd completely spoil us, like we imagine grandmas are supposed to do. [3]_____ She also looked like my idea of a typical granny: she was old, white-haired and wrinkly.

[4]_____ Contrary to the common stereotype, the average age for becoming a grandparent is still only 51 in the UK and 48 in the States. However, compared with our grandparents, we're fitter and will live longer, which means we can potentially play a more active role in helping with childcare. With more women working and with the costs of childcare rising, it's estimated that almost 20% of grandparents now look after grandchildren for more than ten hours a week. [5]_____ All of this poses a problem for women like me

who fought for the freedom to get out of the home and have a career: we want our daughters to have the same freedom to work, but are reluctant to give up our own jobs in order to help them. We might provide financial support instead, but again that might mean making sacrifices, such as spending less on the leisure and travel we enjoy so much.

On top of this, my notion that the role of grandparents is to be indulgent also seems to be problematic. It's true that many grandparents today are often reluctant to discipline their grandchildren because it breaks the unspoken rule that grandparents should never interfere with their children's parenting. Yet at the same time, it's fairly obvious that a lack of discipline can produce spoilt children who rule the house. [6]_____

Still, while there are complications, research also suggests there'll be benefits for me in the longer relationship I'll have with my grandson. A study in *Contemporary Grandparenting* found that such relationships are stronger and more two-way than we perhaps realise. [7]_____ However, research suggests that grandchildren increasingly contribute to the relationship by helping their grandparents stay up-to-date with changes in the world and 'keeping them young'. Now that's something I'd certainly feel good about.

3 Read the article. Find out:

1 what reasons the writer gives to explain why she's struggling with her new role.

2 how she feels about being referred to as Granny – and why.

3 which of her grandparents she knew best.

4 two stereotypes of grandparents that are mentioned.

5 how the writer might benefit from her relationship with her grandson.

6 why the writer mentions each of the words in Exercise 2.

4 Work in pairs. Put the missing sentences below in the correct place (1–7) in the article. There is one sentence you do not need.

a Perhaps unsurprisingly, though, many say they'd prefer to do less.

b In China, they even have a name for this phenomenon – 'Little Emperors'.

c She'd take us to the circus, buy us sweets and cook us our favourite meals.

d The name just doesn't seem right.

e We typically think it's grandparents that give most, whether that be money, love or wisdom.

f I can't be alone in having these mixed and complex feelings.

g Grandparents like travelling too.

h I'd sometimes even open the tin when he wasn't there to smell it.

5 Each group of phrases (1–8) has the same word missing. Find the mising words in the article.

1 have vague ~ of / have some wonderful ~ of / one of my earliest ~ is of

2 ~ to what most people believe / ~ to the stereotype / ~ to what you may have heard

3 ~ to him, I'm doing well / ~ to our grandparents, we're fitter / ~ to other countries

4 play an active ~ in their lives / play a minor ~ / the traditional ~ of the husband

5 it's ~ that 30% of grandparents work / it's ~ that fewer than one in six men help in the house

6 they gave me the ~ to choose / they're restricting our ~ / fight for the ~ to have a career

7 they're ~ to help / he was ~ to leave / we're ~ to give up our freedom

8 ~ to the relationship / all our kids ~ to the housework / he didn't ~ much to the discussion

6 Write four true sentences using phrases from Exercise 5. Then work in groups and share your ideas.

One of my earliest memories is of sitting on my grandmother's knee. It was a sunny day and we were outside under a tree somewhere.

SPEAKING

7 The article is mainly about the UK. Work in groups. Discuss how similar or different things are in your country. Talk about the following:

• the age of grandparents

• the role of grandparents

• childcare – the cost and who does it

GRAMMAR

> ### Used to, would and past simple
> When we talk about our memories, we can use *used to* and *would* as well as the past simple.

8 Look at these sentences from the article. Answer the questions below.

a *He often **smoked** a pipe.*

b *I **used to love** the smell of the fresh tobacco. I**'d** sometimes even **open** the tin when he **wasn't** there to smell it.*

c *After he **died**, Gran **moved** to a town by the seaside and we**'d go** and **visit** her each summer.*

d *She **was** old, white-haired and wrinkly.*

1 Which forms in bold show a habit or regular event in the past?

2 Do you know how to form the negative of *used to*?

3 Which forms are used to talk about a past state, such as having, liking and being?

4 Which form do we use to talk about single events in the past?

G Check your ideas on page 90 and do Exercise 1.

9 Complete the texts with one word in each space. Contractions count as one word.

1 My brother used to [1]_____ really naughty when he [2]_____ younger. He [3]_____ write on the walls and he [4]_____ never do what my parents told him. He often [5]_____ fights at school too.

2 We used [1]_____ go camping a lot when I [2]_____ a kid. We usually [3]_____ by the beach. We'd [4]_____ swimming every day and do lots of sunbathing. One year, we [5]_____ to Slovakia and [6]_____ a week there.

10 Work in pairs. Tell your partner about two of the things below. Try to give an example of one particular incident you remember.

• your memories of a grandparent

• someone you know whose character has changed

• your memories of summer holidays with family

• a free-time activity you no longer do

• the lunch break when you were at primary school

HOW DO YOU KNOW EACH OTHER?

SPEAKING

1 Work in groups. Talk about how you got to know two of your closest friends and, if you have one, your girlfriend / boyfriend or partner. Use some of the language below.

- We grew up together.
- We met at primary / secondary school.
- We met at university / work.
- We met through a friend.
- We met at a party.
- It's a long story!

LISTENING

2 ▶ 58 Listen to five people talking about how they know a Belgian man called Nicolas. Match each speaker (1–5) to one of the sentences below. There is one sentence you do not need.

a They met while travelling round a country.

b He / She shared a bad experience with Nicolas.

c They didn't like each other to begin with.

d He / She fell out with a friend of Nicolas's.

e She's an ex-girlfriend of Nicolas's.

f She's going out with Nicolas.

3 ▶ 58 Listen again. Are the sentences true (T) or false (F)?

1 a Nicolas once spent a summer working as a waiter.
  b He complained to his boss in the café about the way he was being treated.

2 a Sandra remembers him as a very outgoing person.
  b Sandra is glad they split up.

3 a Nicolas and Shane, the friend he met while travelling, are very different to each other.
  b Two years ago, Shane visited Nicolas from Australia.

4 a Brigitta, his girlfriend, thinks Nicolas has a very different character to her.
  b She made the first move in their relationship.

5 a Franck, Jef and Nicolas used to live together.
  b Franck regrets he's no longer friends with Jef.

4 Work in pairs. Discuss the questions.

- Why do you think Sandra (his ex-girlfriend) and Brigitta (his current girlfriend) have such different views of Nicolas?

- Do you think you show different sides of your personality in different situations? Give examples.

- Do you think you've changed in the last year? The last five years? The last ten years?

- Have you ever fallen out with anyone? When? Why? Are you friends again now?

4 I wish I'd tried harder at school.

5 I really wish we hadn't moved house.

6 Honestly, I wish I hadn't said anything.

7 I wish I hadn't gone to the meeting.

8 I sometimes wish they'd given me a different name.

PRONUNCIATION

7 ▶ 59 Listen to the sentences in Exercise 6. Notice that in natural speech, the '*d*' in *I'd* and the '*t*' in *hadn't* are hardly heard at all. Practise saying the sentences as quickly as you can.

8 Write three sentences about things you wish you had / hadn't done in the past. Then work in groups and talk about your regrets.

G For further practice, see Exercise 2 on page 90.

VOCABULARY Relationships

9 Check you understand the phrases in bold. Then put the lines into the correct order to make two stories.

Story 1

a We **were very close** at secondary school.

b so I made new friends and we slowly **drifted apart**.

c Then he **started dating** this girl and he spent more time with her

d but I can't remember the last time we **met up**.

e We still **keep in touch** via Facebook from time to time,

f We used to **hang out** all the time together.

Story 2

g A few years later, I **bumped into he**r through work.

h and I **ended up removing her** from all my social media.

i We were friends for a while before I went to university,

j and we've **remained friends** ever since.

k but then we **fell out over** something stupid

l At first it was **awkward** but then we actually **got on really well**

10 Work in groups. Discuss the questions.

- Who did you hang out with when you started secondary school? What did you do? Have you remained friends? Why? / Why not?

- Have you ever been close to someone but then drifted apart? Do you regret it?

- How many people do you keep in touch with? How? How often do you actually meet up?

- Have you ever removed anyone from your social media? Why?

- Can you think of any friends who fell out? Why? Did they become friends again? Did it cause any awkward moments?

GRAMMAR

Expressing regret using *wish*

5 Look at these sentences from the listening. Complete the rules in the Grammar box below.

a *I sometimes **wish** we**'d stayed** together.*

b *I **wish** we **hadn't split up**.*

To express regret about things in the ¹_____ , we use *wish* + ²_____ tense. To express regret about things that didn't happen, but that we wanted to happen, we use *wish* + ³_____ + past participle. To express regret about things that did happen, but that we didn't want to happen, we use *wish* + ⁴_____ + past participle.

G Check your ideas on page 90 and do Exercise 1.

6 Work in pairs. Think of possible things that were said before / after these sentences.

For number 1, maybe it was something like this: 'I asked her out on a date, but then she told me she was married. I wish I'd known before I asked her! I felt so stupid.'

1 I wish I'd known.

2 I wish I'd met him.

3 I wish they'd told me earlier.

GREATEST JOURNEY

1 **Read the introduction to the video and check you understand the words and phrases in bold.**

It is widely accepted that the human race originally came from Africa and **migrated** round the whole world, but less is known about the routes our **ancestors** took to reach where we all live now. National Geographic's *Genographic Project* aims to **trace** those routes by collecting **DNA samples** like those being taken in the photo from thousands of people in 400 countries, from the smallest village to the largest cities. Working with IBM, the samples are analysed through a process called *computational biology*, which **reveals** the **genes** in our DNA that people from very different places share. The **goal** of the project is to **unlock the secret** of the connections between us and to show how they go right back to the **distant past**.

2 **Work in pairs. Discuss the questions.**
- Why else might someone have a DNA sample taken?
- What other secrets might DNA reveal about someone?
- Have you heard any news stories about DNA?

3 ▶️ **23** **Watch the video about the Genographic Project and four Americans who took a DNA test in New York's Grand Central Station. Match the words and phrases that you hear with the people.**

1 Didi, Minneapolis	3 Cecille, New York
2 Frank, California	4 J. W., Brooklyn

a adaptable	g New York City cop
b Aztec blood	h people person
c The Bering Strait	i proud
d cultivation of crops	j South East Asia
e killed them	k stone blades
f Middle East	l Spanish

4 **Work in pairs. Explain how the words and phrases in Exercise 3 are connected to the people and what they said.**

5 ▶️ **23** **Which people see a connection between their ancient ancestors and their lives now or their immediate family? In what way? Watch the video again to check your ideas.**

6 **Work in groups. Discuss the questions.**
- Is there much interest in family history in your country? Why do you think that is?
- How much do you know about your great-grandparents and your great-great grandparents?
- Can you trace your family back further? Would you like to know more? Why? / Why not?

UNDERSTANDING FAST SPEECH

7 ▶️ **24** **Read and listen to this extract from the video said at natural pace and then slowed down. To help you, groups of words are marked with / and pauses are marked //. Stressed sounds are in CAPITALS.**

YOU STARt OFF // in AFrica // ALL those YEARS aGO / just like EVerybody ELSE / ALL over the WORLD // AND aROUND / FORty-FIVE THOUsand years aGO / after LIving in AFrica / for a VERY LONG TIME / a LIttle GROUP / of YOUR ANcestors // LEFT AFrica / and MOVEd up into the MIddle EAST

8 **Now you have a go! Practice saying the extract at natural pace.**

REVIEW 6

GRAMMAR

1 Complete the text with one word in each space.

I ¹_____ up in the countryside and me and my younger brother ²_____ to love looking for animals. We ³_____ go into the forest and the fields trying to find things. We ⁴_____ to be careful, though, because there were some dangerous things out there. My brother ⁵_____ once bitten by a snake and nearly died, but luckily we ⁶_____ to get him to a doctor just in time. I wish I'd taken better care of him, but back then I ⁷_____ used to worry about things like that. For special festivals, animals ⁸_____ killed and eaten. The first time I saw an animal get killed, I was so shocked I could ⁹_____ speak! Most people have stopped killing their own animals, though, as good quality meat can ¹⁰_____ bought everywhere these days.

2 Complete the second sentence so that it has a similar meaning to the first sentence using the word given. Do not change the word given. You must use between three and four words, including the word given.

1 We've redecorated the flat since the last time you visited.
The flat _____ you last visited. **SINCE**

2 You'll need to pay the full fee before you arrive.
The full fee _____ in advance. **SHOULD**

3 I had really long hair when I was younger.
I _____ really long hair when I was younger. **TO**

4 They usually collect the rubbish every Wednesday.
The rubbish _____ every Wednesday. **NORMALLY**

5 It was so cold that I lost all feeling in my hands.
It was so cold that I _____ my hands at all. **NOT**

6 It's a shame I didn't practise more when I was younger.
I _____ more when I was younger. **WISH**

3 Choose the correct option.

1 I had such a bad cold that I *could / couldn't* hardly speak.

2 I wish I *wouldn't have / hadn't* mentioned it to anyone now.

3 I looked everywhere, but I *didn't manage / managed not* to find it.

4 I applied for about 50 jobs and in the end I *managed to / could* find one.

5 To be honest, I regret *to tell / telling* my parents about it.

6 My grandfather *used to / would* be very direct. He always said what he meant!

7 Something really strange *was happened / happened* to me yesterday.

8 I *went / used to go* to Texas for a month with my parents when I was eleven.

4 ▶ 60 Listen and write the six sentences you hear.

VOCABULARY

5 Match the verbs (1–8) with the collocates (a–h).

1 overcome	a a dreadful noise
2 set	b over money
3 fall out	c a target
4 get	d the pain
5 take	e upset easily
6 make	f barriers
7 reach	g things personally
8 get through	h the summit

6 Complete the sentences with the best prepositions.

1 I've been really stressing _____ how I'm going to find a job after university.

2 I like being able to play an active role _____ my grandchildren's lives.

3 I'm trying to get fit at the moment. I've set myself a target _____ running five kilometres a day.

4 I managed to get top grades in the test. I'm quite proud _____ myself.

5 We could hear this strange noise _____ the distance. It was quite scary.

7 Complete the sentences. Use the word in brackets to form a word that fits in the space.

1 He's very _____ . I mean, he makes things, he writes a lot and he plays the violin. (create)

2 He was born without legs and yet he's managed to overcome severe _____ and become a well-respected politician. (able)

3 My sister is always very _____ . I mean, she really hates losing. (compete)

4 She's really _____ . She really pushes herself. She's going to go a long way. (ambition)

5 He's a great player. He has this real _____ to win. (determined)

6 To be good at tennis, I think you need to very intense and very _____ . (focus)

8 Complete the text with one word in each space. The first letters are given.

We were best friends at school. I mean, we were very ¹cl_____ . We used to ²ha_____ out together a lot. She was very ³br_____ , very smart and I respected that. She's from a poor family, but she managed to ⁴ov_____ poverty and become very successful. She once told me that she'd always ⁵dr_____ of becoming a lawyer and she managed to reach that ⁶go_____ and make her dream ⁷c_____ true.

Despite her achievements, though, she was always very ⁸mo_____ – she never showed off or anything. However, she started ⁹da_____ this guy I didn't like and our lives went in different directions. I tried to talk about it with her once, but she's incredibly ¹⁰se_____ and took it badly. She saw it as a personal attack. She ¹¹re_____ me from her social media and we haven't talked for ages. The thing is, though, she'll be at an old friend's wedding this weekend and I'm really hoping it won't be too ¹²aw_____ or difficult!

JOURNEYS

SPEAKING

1 Imagine you are the man in the photo. Think about the questions below.

- Who are you? What do you do?
- Where are you from? Where are you trying to get to?
- What's happened? Why?
- What are you going to do next?

2 Work in pairs. Take turns to tell your stories. Your partner should sympathise and ask extra questions.

3 Work with a new partner. Discuss the questions.

- Do you usually take a lot of luggage on holiday or do you travel light? Why?
- Do you know anyone who has spent a few months travelling? Where did they go?
- What's the longest journey you've ever taken? How long did it take door-to-door?

HOW WAS YOUR JOURNEY?

VOCABULARY Ways of travelling and travel problems

1   Put the words in the box under the correct heading in the table. Some words can go under more than one heading.

tyre	security	line	crossing
traffic lights	take-off	carriage	deck
platform	bend	harbour	check-in desk

By train	By ferry	By car	By plane

2   Work in pairs. Add two more words to each group in the table.

3   Complete the sentences with nouns from Exercise 1.

1   I was waiting on the wrong _____ and so I ended up missing my train!

2   The sea was really rough. It was pouring with rain and very windy, so we couldn't go out on _____ .

3   We got a flat _____ on the motorway and had to stop and change it.

4   I hate flying. I get really anxious – especially during _____ and landing.

5   Last time we came over it was quite rough, but this time we had a very smooth _____ . It was lovely.

6   There'd been a terrible storm and there were trees on the _____ , so the train was delayed for ages.

7   I got stopped going through _____ and they confiscated a little penknife that I'd forgotten to take out of my bag.

8   It was terrifying. The taxi driver overtook another car on quite a tight _____ . You couldn't see if anyone was coming in the opposite direction.

4   Work in pairs. Look at the photos. Discuss what is good and what is bad about each way of travelling. Which way do you prefer? Why?

LISTENING

5   ▶ 61 Listen to two conversations about journeys and answer the questions.

1   How did the people in each conversation travel?

2   What three problems did each have?

6   ▶ 61 Can you remember what these adjectives were used to describe? Work in pairs and compare your ideas. Then listen again and check.

Conversation 1: huge   bumpy   terrifying

Conversation 2: slippery   wrong   stupid   hurt

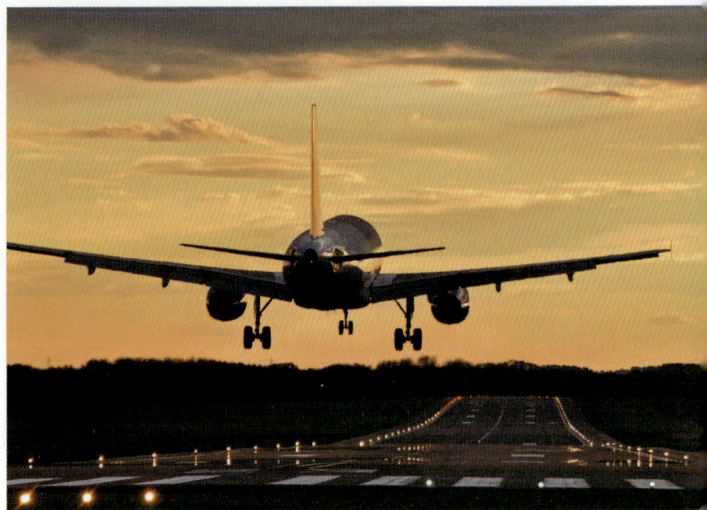

7 Work in groups. Discuss the questions.

- How long before your flight do you usually get to the airport? Why?
- Have you ever missed a flight? Why?
- Has anything strange or scary ever happened to you while flying / driving?
- Can you drive? What are your strong points and weak points as a driver?
- Do you agree with Lara's comments about male drivers?

DEVELOPING CONVERSATIONS

How come?

In conversations, we often use *How come ...?* instead of *Why ...?*

K: *I had a bit of a nightmare getting here.*

L: *Oh really?* **How come?**

Notice that after *How come* we use sentence order rather than question order:

Why was it so busy? → *How come* **it was so busy?**

Why didn't you take the train? → *How come* **you didn't take the train?**

8 Complete the sentences with *how come* or *why*.

1 So _____ it took you so long to get here?

2 _____ was the plane delayed?

3 So _____ you left the car at home?

4 _____ you know so much about trains?

5 _____ are you going to Vietnam, then?

6 _____ they've decided to move to Australia?

9 Work in pairs. Take turns asking and answering the questions from Exercise 8.

10 Work with a new partner. Ask your partner four questions starting *How come ...?*

UNDERSTANDING VOCABULARY

Phrasal verbs

A phrasal verb is a verb (*put*, *throw*, *take*, etc.) plus a particle (*up*, *off*, *out*, *down*, etc.) Often the meaning is not obviously connected to either the verb or the particle. For example, when a plane *takes off,* it's not taking anything and it goes up into the sky!

When you translate phrasal verbs, you may use just one word in your language, while others may be translated into a phrase.

Phrasal verbs appear in all kinds of text – formal and informal, written and spoken – but are more common in speaking. Learn them as you would any other verb: for example, in groups connected to a topic or as they appear in a text. Notice collocations and other phrases connected to each phrasal verb.

11 Replace the words in italics in the sentences with the phrasal verbs that were used in the conversations. Then look at Track 61 on page 104 and compare your ideas.

1 Andre didn't want to spend too long *sitting, waiting and not doing much* at the airport.

2 I don't want to *experience* that again, I can tell you!

3 Do you want to go and get something to eat, or do you want to *register* at the hotel first?

4 Well, to begin with, it was still dark when I *started my journey.*

5 And then it immediately started to *rain very heavily,* so the roads were really slippery.

6 I couldn't *find an answer to the problem of* where I was or where I was going!

7 When I finally *returned* onto the right road, I almost had an accident.

8 I did have to stop and park the car for a few minutes to *stop feeling so angry and upset.*

12 Add the missing particle to these sentences.

1 We set at five in the morning, so I'm exhausted.

2 We didn't have to queue because we checked online.

3 We had to hang at the station for an hour because my mum couldn't pick us up till four.

4 I was exhausted. I left home at six in the morning and I didn't get till ten at night.

5 My child got into a panic and she wouldn't calm.

6 We went absolute hell to get here, I can tell you!

7 I was totally lost. I couldn't work where I was.

8 It started to pour halfway there. We were absolutely soaked by the time we arrived.

13 Work in pairs. Answer the questions.

1 What's the opposite of setting off?

2 Can you think of three different times when you might need to check in?

3 Can you think of three places where you might have to hang around? Why?

4 Can you think of three situations when you might need to tell someone to calm down?

5 Can you think of three different things you might go through in life?

CONVERSATION PRACTICE

14 You are going to talk about a terrible journey. First, think about how to describe the journey using vocabulary from this lesson. Invent details if you need to. Next, work in pairs. Take it in turns to tell your stories. Remember to react to the stories and to ask follow-up questions.

🎥 25 To watch the video and do the activities, see the DVD ROM.

A BRAND NEW START

READING

1 Work in pairs. Think of five different reasons why people might decide to leave their country. Then discuss the questions.

- Do you know anyone who has moved to another country? Which one? Why?
- Would you like to live in another country? If yes, which one? Why? If not, what might make you?

2 Read the first three paragraphs of the article below. Find out:

1 where the people in the photo are from and where they are trying to get to.
2 why Hussain Bashardost made this journey.
3 what difficulties he faced on his journey.
4 what happened to him in the end.

3 Work in pairs. Discuss why the numbers and things below were mentioned. Read the article again and check your ideas.

1 sixteen	6 four times
2 $5,000	7 three days
3 one bedroom	8 400 people
4 ten	9 80 hours
5 eight other people	10 nine months

4 Work in groups. Discuss the questions.

- What problems do you think Hussain faced once he was given asylum in Australia?
- In what ways do you think the experience of his journey was an advantage to him?

5 Read paragraphs 4–6 of the article. Decide if the sentences are true (T) or false (F). Underline the parts of the article that support your answers.

1 Hussain works for a small printing company.
2 He has no regrets about leaving Afghanistan.
3 Businesses started by immigrants don't generate much money.
4 The journeys made by refugees often make them more afraid of risk.
5 The journeys can help refugees get better at making deals.
6 The writer is critical of the way immigration is often discussed.

6 Work in pairs. Look at the words and phrases in bold in the two parts of the article. Decide what they mean from the context.

THE LONG JOURNEY TO A NEW LIFE

Darrell Banks considers the positive impact Australia's boat people can make

While most people entering Australia arrive at one of the country's international airports, relaxed after a comfortable flight, for some the journey is far longer and involves dangers most of us can hardly imagine. Take Hussain Bashardost, for example. A member of the Hazara **ethnic minority**, often targeted and treated badly in their native Afghanistan, Hussain was just sixteen when his family decided that it was in the interests of his own safety to get him out of the country. He was driven to Kabul, the capital, where a family friend paid an organised gang $5,000 to get him to Australia.

Hussain was then flown to Jakarta in Indonesia. He was met at the airport by a man who took him to a tiny one-bedroom apartment, where he lived for the next ten months with eight other asylum seekers – some Afghan, some Iranian – all waiting; waiting to hear that their boat was ready to leave. Four times he was driven in an overcrowded truck to the south coast of Java; four times he was squeezed into a fishing boat that really didn't look as if it would last three days at sea, let alone hold 400 people, and four times he ended up back in Jakarta after being caught by the local police. If he hadn't been so **determined**, Hussain could easily have given up and returned home.

Eventually, though, a boat managed to **set sail** and after 80 terrifying hours on heavy seas, they finally landed on Christmas Island, Australia's most northerly territory. He had survived in some of the most hazardous waters on Earth, but his **ordeal** was not yet over. Hussain was then kept in a government **detention centre** for another nine months before finally being allowed to stay in the country he now calls home.

46

7 Work in groups. Discuss the questions.

- Do you know what kind of restrictions on immigration there are in your country?
- Can you think of any famous immigrants into your country? What difference have they made?
- Can you think of any famous people from your country who have moved abroad?

GRAMMAR

Third conditionals

We use third conditionals to talk about imagined situations in the past. They usually have two parts: an *if*-clause referring to the situation and a second clause showing results or consequences.

8 Look at these sentences from the article. Answer the questions below.

a *If he **hadn't been** so determined, Hussain **could** easily **have given up** and returned home.*

b *If I**'d stayed** in Afghanistan, none of this **would've happened**.*

1 What structure is used in the *if*-clauses?
2 Which two modal verbs are used in the other clauses?
3 What structure follows the modal verbs?
4 What really happened in each situation?

G Check your ideas on page 91 and do Exercise 1.

9 Match the two parts of the sentences.

1 The economy would've collapsed
2 If it hadn't been for the war,
3 If I hadn't had that teacher,
4 If we'd left a bit earlier,
5 The team might have won
6 I'd never have met my wife

a I probably would never have gone to university.
b if I hadn't gone to that party.
c if all the players had been fit.
d if the government hadn't helped the banks.
e we would've stayed in our own country.
f we might not have missed the train.

10 Work in pairs. Think of alternative endings for 1–6 in Exercise 9.

11 Think of three important moments in your life. Then write three third conditional sentences to show how things could / would have been different if they had never happened.

12 Work in groups. Explain your sentences to each other in as much detail as you can.

After I graduated from university, I spent six months travelling around Latin America. One day I was on a bus in Chile and I got talking to the guy next to me – and he ended up becoming my husband. We would never have met if I hadn't decided to go travelling.

G For further practice, see Exercise 2 on page 91.

So was it all worth it? 'Absolutely,' Hussain tells me when I meet him in the office of his printing company that now employs six people and has **an annual turnover** of $500,000. 'If I'd stayed in Afghanistan, none of this would've happened. At best, my life would've been incredibly hard and I would've **struggled** to have even a basic standard of living. I'm not saying life here has been easy, but at least Australia has given me a chance and I hope your readers can see I'm now paying the country back.'

In fact, Hussain is part of a global trend that has attracted the attention of researchers. A number of recent studies agree that immigrants – and in particular immigrants who have **fled** their own countries – are more likely to start their own businesses than locals, with these businesses then **making considerable contributions** to the national economies. Theories as to why this might be vary. One idea is that refugees are less worried about risk, as they have already risked everything on their journeys out of their own countries. Secondly, refugees are also often well connected, and may well have friends and families in countries all over the world. Thirdly, they may lack the necessary language skills or qualifications needed to succeed locally and so decide to set up on their own. Finally, they often possess excellent negotiating skills, which they have had to develop on their journeys here.

Such skill sets are often forgotten among all the political debate on the subject of immigration as, of course, is the fact that most refugees have risked their lives many times over to be where they are today. Maybe it's time to recognise it's not just individuals that mature and grow **thanks to** immigration – it's nations as well.

IT'S MY OWN FAULT

SPEAKING

1 **Work in groups. Discuss the questions.**

- How do you usually react when things go wrong? Do you do any of the following?
  - I often panic.
  - I go very quiet.
  - I'm very relaxed. I usually believe the situation will sort itself out.
  - I usually organise people and focus on solutions.
  - I blame myself.
- Who's the best / worst person you know in a crisis?
- Give an example of a time something went wrong in these contexts. What happened? How did you react?
  - on holiday
  - at work or college
  - making or repairing something

LISTENING

2 ▶ **62** **Listen to four conversations about things going wrong on holiday. Match each conversation (1–4) to one of the problems below. There are two problems you do not need.**

a There was a problem going through security.

b They had a problem with the heat.

c There was a problem at check-in.

d They had a problem with the accommodation.

e There was a problem with what they packed.

f They got a rash on their skin from insect bites.

3 ▶ **62** **Match these verbs to the nouns they were used with in the conversations. Then listen again and check your answers.**

check	choose	go	have
pay	put on	stay	weigh

1 _____ the forecast

2 _____ an amazing time

3 _____ in a little place

4 _____ the first cheap place we came across

5 _____ purple

6 _____ some sun cream

7 _____ your bags

8 _____ an excess baggage charge

4 **Work in pairs. Discuss the questions.**

- Have you ever had bad weather on holiday?
- Have you ever had to complain about a hotel or place you stayed in? If yes, what about?
- Do you like to spend time in the sun? Why? / Why not?
- Do you ever travel on low-cost airlines? What do you have to pay extra for?

UNDERSTANDING VOCABULARY

5 **Complete the exchanges with a basic adjective and its corresponding extreme adjective. You may need to change the order of the adjectives.**

angry – furious	hungry – starving
wet – soaked	interesting – fascinating
crowded – packed	tasty – delicious
dirty – filthy	tired – exhausted

1 A: How did you find the museum? It was absolutely _____ when we went!
  B: It was busy, but it wasn't too _____ .

2 A: You must be _____ they've lost your luggage.
  B: Yeah, I am. I'm absolutely _____ !

3 A: You must be _____ after such a long journey.
  B: I am a bit _____ but I actually slept on the plane for a while.

4 A: You must be _____ after such a long journey.
  B: I am. I'm absolutely _____ . Have you got anything to eat?

5 A: How was the journey back? Did you get _____ in that storm?
  B: We got absolutely _____ ! I didn't have an umbrella or anything.

6 A: Did you like the food? I thought it was absolutely _____ .
  B: Yeah, it was quite _____ , but I've had better.

7 A: The place we stayed in was a bit _____ .
  B: A bit? It was absolutely _____ ! I couldn't believe it.

8 A: I've heard Tabriz is a very _____ city.
  B: Yeah, it is. It's _____ . It has so much history!

PRONUNCIATION

6 ▶ 63 Listen to the exchanges in Exercise 5. Mark the main stress in the extreme adjectives and notice the intonation.

7 Work in pairs. Practise reading out the exchanges. Try to give emphasis to the extreme adjectives.

8 Work in groups. Tell each other as much as you can about places you have been to that were: *boiling, fascinating, filthy, freezing* or *packed*.

GRAMMAR

Should have

We use *should (not) have* + past participle to talk about things that went wrong in the past.

9 Look at these sentences from the conversations. Answer the questions below each one.

a *We **should've looked** around more.*

1 Did they check lots of places?

2 Was that the right decision? Why? / Why not?

b *I **shouldn't have stayed** in the sun for so long.*

3 Did the speaker stay in the sun a long time?

4 Was that a good idea? Why? / Why not?

G Check your ideas on page 91 and do Exercise 1.

10 Work in pairs. Imagine what actually happened in 1–6 below. Then use a third conditional to explain what would have been a better idea.

I knew we should've taken the plane instead of the ferry.

We took the ferry, but it took ages and the sea was really rough as well. If we'd taken the plane, we would've got there a lot quicker.

1 I should've worn something lighter.

2 He shouldn't have been driving so fast in the rain.

3 You should've read the instructions more carefully.

4 I knew we should've booked the tickets in advance.

5 His parents shouldn't have left him on his own at home.

6 I shouldn't have left my bag hanging from the back of my seat.

11 Work in groups. Read the situations in File 11 on page 97. Which group can write the most *should've / shouldn't have* sentences about each situation?

G For further practice, see Exercise 2 on page 91.

DEVELOPING CONVERSATIONS

Blaming people

We use *it's my / his fault* or *I blame myself / him* to say who caused a problem. We often use *should have* and third conditionals as well.

12 Complete the sentences with one word in each space.

1 Don't _____ me. You _____'ve read the small print.

2 It's not _____ fault we're late. If you hadn't _____ so long to get ready, we would _____ caught the train.

3 It's not my fault – it's _____ ! You were the one who was driving. You should've _____ more careful.

4 If you ask me, it's your airline's _____ . They _____ have waited for you for one more minute.

5 I _____ myself. I should've listened to my dad. If I _____ done what he said, none of this would've happened.

6 The problem could _____ happened to anyone. It's nobody's _____ . It's just one of those things that happen.

13 Work in pairs. You are going to roleplay a conversation. Choose one of the situations from Exercise 11. Decide who will take which role and think about how you will try to blame the other person.

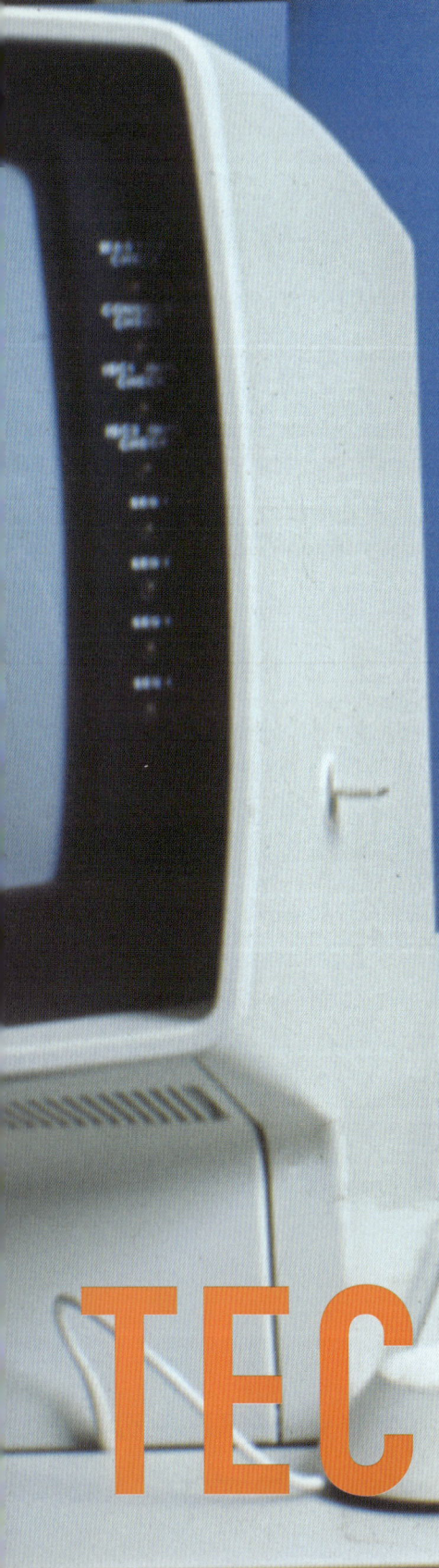

TECHNOLOGY

- talk about computers
- explain and sort out problems
- describe games
- discuss issues around computer gaming
- talk about apps and gadgets

SPEAKING

1 **Work in pairs. Discuss the questions.**

- When do you think this photo was taken?
- What do you think the equipment in the photo is and what is it for?
- How have computers changed since you first started using them?
- What do you think has been the most significant change? Why?

2 **Work with a new partner. Discuss the questions.**

- Which of the following do you have: a desktop? a laptop? a tablet? a smartphone?
- Which make/s do you have? Why did you choose them? Are you happy with them?
- Which of these things do you use computers to help you do? How good are you at each one?
  - prepare presentations
  - design things
  - edit videos
  - manage accounts
  - hold video meetings
  - code new programmes
- What else do you use your computer for at work, when studying and in your free time?

MY COMPUTER HATES ME

VOCABULARY Computers

1 **Label the picture with these words.**

cable	external hard drive	mouse	scanner	cursor	keyboard
plug	socket	file	menu	printer	screen

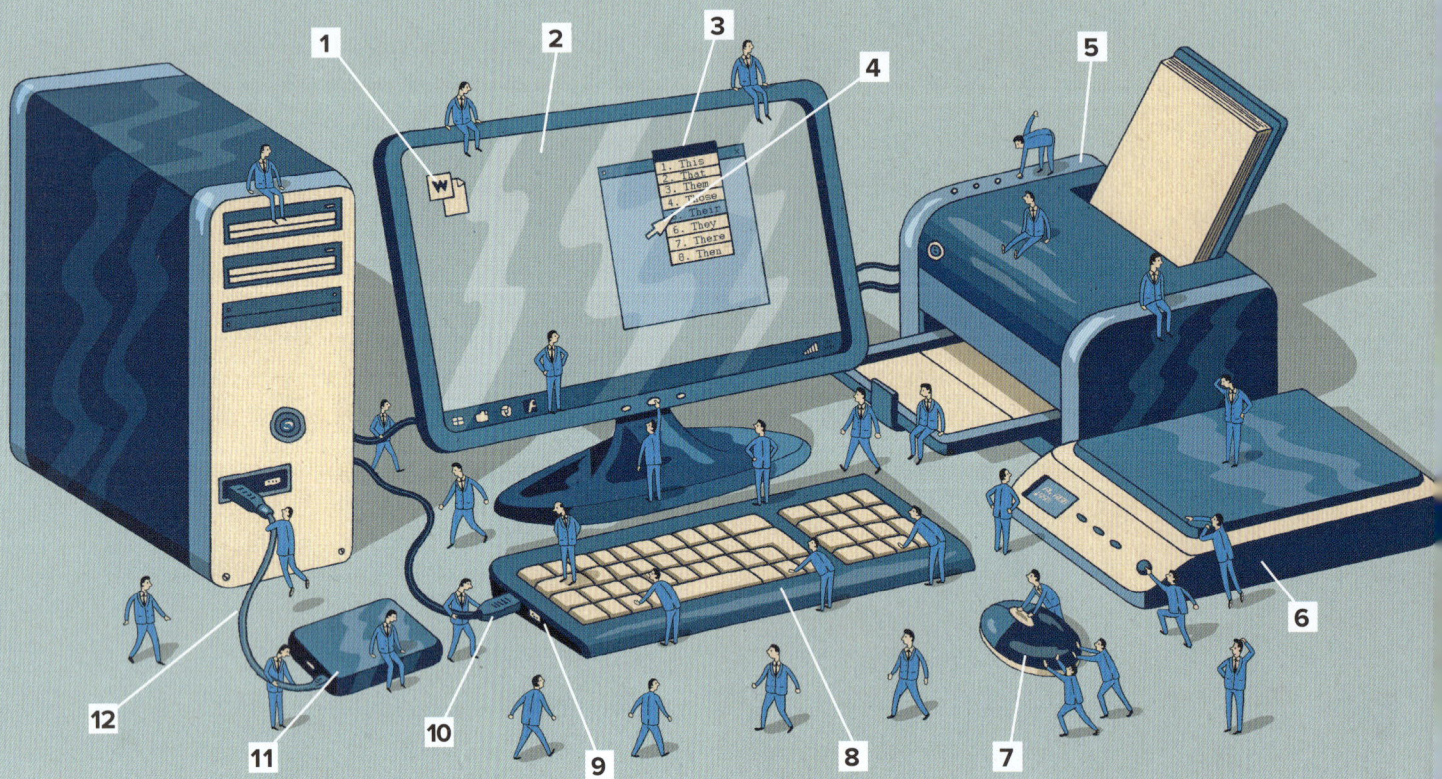

2 **Complete the sentences with words from Exercise 1.**

1 I can click on the icon and see the drop-down _____ , but then when I try to select one of the options, nothing!

2 The reason it's running so slowly is because the memory's almost full. You ought to move some of your files to an _____ to free up some space.

3 You need to check your connections again. Maybe you've plugged something into the wrong _____ .

4 The _____ isn't working. I don't know why. Maybe it needs more ink or something.

5 I tripped over a _____ on the floor and managed to knock the whole computer over.

6 You need to move the _____ over the image and then the instructions should come up.

7 I might be wrong, but it sounds like the _____ on your power cable isn't properly connected.

8 I'm not sure why, but my _____ isn't working. It was fine yesterday, but I've just tried to scan a picture in and I'm not getting anything.

9 Next time, remember to make a backup copy of the _____ . Copy it to the Cloud once it's done.

10 My computer crashed and when I rebooted it, the _____ was completely blank.

3 **Which of the sentences in Exercise 2 were said by someone who works on an IT help desk and which were said by someone calling the help desk?**

4 **Work in pairs. Think of six more problems you could have with some of the things from Exercise 1.**

5 **Work in groups. Check you understand the words and phrases in bold in the sentences below. Then discuss the questions.**

1 Can you think of three other things you can **click on**, apart from **icons**?

2 To **free up space** where else could you move files to, apart from an external hard drive?

3 Can you think of two other reasons why computers **run slowly**? What's the best solution?

4 Can you think of four things you **plug in**?

5 Can you think of any other reasons why a mouse might **not work properly**?

6 What else might you want to **scan in**, apart from a picture? Why?

LISTENING

6 ▶ 64 Listen to four phone calls to an IT help desk. For each call, answer these questions.

1 What's the problem?

2 What advice is given?

7 ▶ 64 Work in pairs. Say which phone call (1–4) you think each sentence is from – and why. Then listen again and check your ideas.

a You're not the worst offender.

b It's stupid of me, I know, but I always forget to copy them.

c Honestly, it's driving me mad!

d That's a disaster!

e It's the age we live in!

f One minute. Let me just have one more look.

g Yeah, try that and see what happens.

h I need these things in plain English, you see!

8 Work in pairs. Discuss the questions.

- Which of the four problems is the most serious? Why?
- What do you think of the advice the IT help desk staff gave?
- Have you ever had any similar problems? If so, when? What happened? Did you sort the problems out? How?
- Do you know anyone who works in IT? Do they enjoy it?
- Would you like to do that kind of work? Why? / Why not?

DEVELOPING CONVERSATIONS

Sorting out problems

There are some common phrases we use when sorting out problems.

A: *All my files have disappeared from the screen.*

B: *Have you tried rebooting at all?*

A: *Yes, I have and it didn't do any good.*

B: *OK. Have you tried searching for specific files by name?*

A: *No, not yet. Should I?*

B: *Yeah, try that and see if anything comes up.*

9 Put the two conversations into the correct order. Notice the phrases in bold.

Conversation 1

a OK. Well, you can't handle that file type, then. **Maybe you should** email the sender and ask them to resend it as a different file type.

b **Have you tried** download**ing** it to your desktop and seeing if you can open it from there?

c **Otherwise, I don't know what else to suggest.**

d **Yeah, but I didn't have any success.**

e I don't know why, but I can't open this file.

f **OK. I'll try that.**

Conversation 2

g **No, not yet. Do you think I should?**

h My boss wants us all to start using this new system, but I don't get how it works.

i **I've tried, but it didn't make any difference.** She just said we all have to switch!

j **Yeah, try it. Otherwise, you're probably best** doing an actual course somewhere.

k **Have you tried** talk**ing** to her about it? **Maybe you should** tell her.

l Wow! **OK. Well, have you** looked on the Internet? There must be videos showing you how to use it somewhere.

PRONUNCIATION

10 ▶ 65 Listen to some of the sentences from Exercise 9. Notice the way the main verbs and nouns are stressed. Then listen again and repeat.

11 Work in pairs. Take turns to say the six problems below and to give advice on them. Use some of the phrases in bold from the box and Exercise 9.

1 The printer's not working.

2 I'm trying to download a file and it's taking forever!

3 I really want to get a new phone, but I can't afford one at the moment.

4 My boss wants me to run our social media campaign, but it's too much responsibility.

5 I found my boyfriend texting other girls.

6 My boss wants me to add him as a friend on Facebook.

CONVERSATION PRACTICE

12 Work in pairs. You are going to roleplay four phone conversations between someone who works on an IT help desk and someone with computer problems. Make a list of as many problems you could have with a computer as you can. Compare your list with another pair. Did they have any ideas you had not thought of?

13 Now roleplay four conversations with your partner. Change roles after each conversation. Use as much language from this lesson as possible.

🔴📹 26 To watch the video and do the activities, see the DVD ROM.

GAMES PEOPLE PLAY

SPEAKING

1 Work in pairs. Discuss the questions.

- How do you feel about computer games?
- Do you ever play them? If so, how often?
- Do you know anyone who is very good at computer games? Which ones?

VOCABULARY Describing games

2 Complete the descriptions by putting the words in brackets into the correct order.

1 It's pretty basic. You move bricks in a wall so you have three or more _____ (in / of / same / the / colour / row / a) and then they disappear. You **advance to the next level by** clearing all the bricks _____ (time / the / out / before / runs).

2 Basically, you _____ (the / role / of / take) an army leader and you **go on a mission to recover** secret papers from the enemy base. _____ (kill / and / you / to / shoot / have) the enemy to reach your goal.

3 Basically, you _____ (build / resources / gather / to) your own city. You can play on your own or **interact with other players**. It's very creative, so _____ (possibilities / endless / the / are).

4 It's a driving game. You select a car and can change it any way that you want to. You can play as one player and **try to beat your best time** or you can _____ (to / opponents / against / race / up / six) live.

5 It _____ (experience / to / you / allows) the daily life of a farmer and you can **make your own modifications**, which is really great. They _____ (the / the / look / game / of / enhance) and make it more realistic.

3 Work in groups. Describe games you know using the phrases in brackets and in bold from Exercise 2.

I sometimes play this game on my iPad called AcChen. You have to find matching pictures and if you can match all the images before the time runs out, then you advance to the next level.

LISTENING

4 ▶ 66 Listen to some news about the gaming industry. Find:

1 an example of how the industry has grown.
2 a prediction about its future.
3 how many people work in the industry.
4 why $500 million and one day are mentioned.
5 a problem that the industry still faces.

5 Work in pairs. Discuss the questions.

- Do you know of any other games that have made huge amounts of money? Have you played them? If you have, what were they like? Would you recommend them?
- How big do you think gaming is in your country? Do you know any locally produced games?
- How many different jobs within the gaming industry can you think of? Do you know anyone who works in the industry? Would you like to? Why? / Why not?
- Do you have any stereotypes of what a typical gamer might be like?

READING

6 Read about three gamers. Match each of the following to the people in the article. Which person:

1 enjoyed the fact that gaming used their imagination?
2 has a large number of fans?
3 finds it funny that consumers get so annoyed about poor service?

MY LIFE AS A GAMER

Martin Percy, Sevenoaks, England

I'm 44 and I'm a computer engineer, so perhaps it's not surprising that I'm such a big gamer. I'm really into simulation games, the kinds of things that let you experience what it's like to do something like fly a plane or drive a huge truck – all from the comfort of your own home. I have my own YouTube channel and I play live to audiences of over 100,000.

I've always been interested in big machinery and the games are incredibly detailed. They feature traffic and buttons and everything, and are very realistic. The feeling of landing a passenger jet safely is incredibly exciting. I also love the social side of it. It enhances the whole experience. I read all the comments from other gamers and enjoy interacting with them.

Contrary to expectations, by the way, I don't live in my parents' basement. I am married, I have three kids and I do have other hobbies as well!

Jessie, Taichung, Taiwan

I got my first desktop when I was at university, and to begin with I wasn't very keen on computer games. The big change came after I graduated and found that I couldn't get a job. I applied for hundreds of different positions and went for a few interviews, but without any success.

Around this time, I discovered *The Sims* and soon I was completely obsessed. I don't know if you know the game or not, but it's quite unusual as there are no fixed objectives; it's more like a virtual world where you can create characters and stories, and so on. I loved the fact it allowed me to be creative. After a while, though, I realised that while I was busy trying to fulfil these fantasy versions of my life, I'd more or less given up on my real life!

4 makes fun of the stereotypes of gamers?

5 found gaming was having a negative impact on their life?

6 is unable to do much online gaming?

7 works in IT?

8 mentions something illegal?

9 had to overcome an addiction?

7 **Work in pairs. Cover the article. Try to remember which verbs went with these words. Then read again and check your ideas.**

1 _____ what it's like to do something

2 _____ traffic and buttons and everything

3 _____ the whole experience

4 _____ characters and stories

5 _____ fantasy versions of my life

6 _____ the habit

7 _____ the kind of games we play

8 _____ money away from designers

9 _____ me laugh

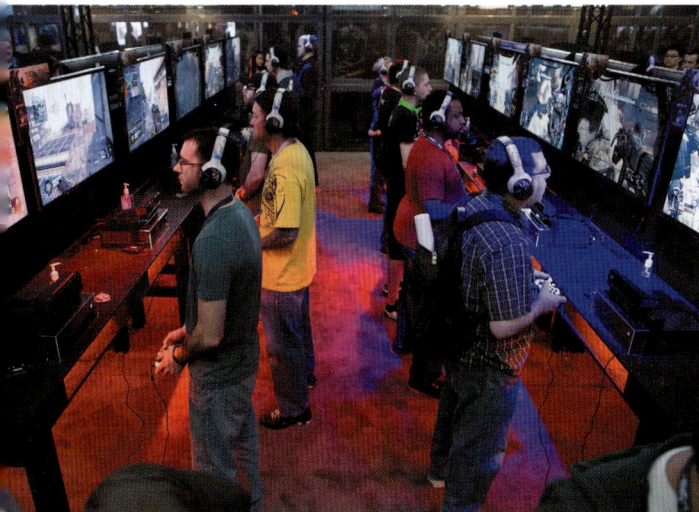

In the end, I decided to quit. It was hard to break the habit, but it's been for the best. I'm working now – for a company that sells household goods – and I've met someone too!

Emerson, Freetown, Sierra Leone

Internet speeds and connections are still a real issue in many areas here, so most of my gaming is done on my smartphone. Obviously, this affects the kind of games we play here. It's not common to play games online with different friends. For us, playing multiplayer just means playing side by side!

Another way in which gaming here is different is the huge number of pirate copies on the market. I'm not saying it's good, because I know that it's taking money away from designers and programmers, but without black market copies, people here could never play most games as they're too expensive.

One other difference here is that we don't get angry like western people. I read recently about all these organised protests in the United States because one part of a game was released later than promised. It made me laugh. Don't get me wrong. I wouldn't be happy in that situation either. It's just that we have bigger things to worry about.

GRAMMAR

Articles

The is known as the definite article. *A / an* are called indefinite articles. In some situations, we don't use any articles at all.

8 **Look at these sentences from the article. Complete the rules below with *the*, *a / an* or *no article*.**

1 *I'm **a computer engineer**.*

2 *I wasn't very keen on **computer games**.*

3 *I've always been interested in **big machinery**.*

4 *I read all **the comments from other gamers**.*

5 *I got my first desktop when I was **at university**.*

6 *I read recently about all these organised protests in **the United States**.*

7 ***The feeling of landing a passenger jet** safely is incredibly exciting.*

8 ***In the end**, I decided to quit.*

a We use _____ :
   - before nouns when they are one of several, when it's not important which one we mean, or when we mention something for the first time.
   - to say what people are.

b We use _____ :
   - before nouns when we think it's clear which thing or things we mean.
   - before some place names.
   - as part of some fixed expressions.

c We use _____ :
   - before uncountable nouns.
   - with plural nouns to talk about things in general.
   - after prepositions in lots of expressions with places.

G Check your ideas on page 92 and do Exercise 1.

9 **Complete the sentences with *a*, *an*, *the* or *X* (= nothing).**

1 _____ use of smartphones in _____ class should be forbidden.

2 _____ computer games can be _____ really good way of learning _____ language.

3 No-one should ever buy _____ pirate copies of _____ computer games or software.

4 I'd never take part in _____ protest about _____ late release of part of _____ game.

5 I'm quite happy with _____ computer that I have at _____ moment.

6 _____ Internet addiction is _____ really serious problem nowadays.

10 **Work in groups. Discuss how far you agree with each of the opinions in Exercise 9. Explain your ideas.**

G For further practice, see Exercise 2 on page 92.

IT'S A NEAT GADGET

SPEAKING

1 **Work in groups. Discuss the questions.**

- Do you know anyone who always buys the latest gadgets, technology or software? Give examples of what they have bought or use.

- Do you know anyone who is a bit of a technophobe?

- Have you bought any new gadgets, apps or software recently? What? Why did you get them?

VOCABULARY Apps and gadgets

2 **Complete each pair of sentences with the same word from the box.**

allows	automatically	built in
interface	recognise	runs

1. a You train it to _____ your voice.
   b If you swipe too fast, it doesn't _____ your fingerprint.

2. a The whole house _____ on solar power.
   b He's got this new bike that _____ on a small battery.

3. a It has a sensor _____ that can tell what temperature it is.
   b The suitcase has GPS _____ , so you can track it wherever it is.

4. a It _____ you to record, edit and share videos.
   b It _____ you to organise meetings, invite people and send reminders.

5. a You set the timer and the heater comes on _____ at whatever time you tell it to.
   b It's amazing. The light just comes on _____ when you open the door.

6. a It's got a very clear user _____ .
   b The _____ isn't very user-friendly. It's quite confusing.

3 **Think of three gadgets, apps or pieces of software that you have. Then work in pairs and tell your partner as much as you can about them using language from Exercise 2.**

LISTENING

4 ▶ **67** **Listen to a podcast where three people review technology. What three apps and gadgets are reviewed?**

5 ▶ **67** **Are the sentences true (T), false (F) or not mentioned (N)? Listen again and check your answers.**

1. The speakers choose the things to review.

2. The cry for help is supposed to scare off attackers in the street.

3. One of the speakers has had their phone stolen.

4. You use the universal translator to translate texts to and from a foreign language.

5. Not all the translations are accurate.

6. James and a friend tried the translator when they went on holiday.

7. It's very easy to fit the remote lock on a door.

8. You need to get an app to use the remote lock.

6 Work in pairs. Discuss the questions.

- What do you think of the three apps and gadgets?
- Do you ever listen to podcasts? What about?
- What things did you find embarrassing when you were a teenager?

GRAMMAR

Infinitive and -ing forms

Verbs can be an infinitive with *to* or an *-ing* form. The choice of form is sometimes decided by rules, but in many cases, there are no rules. It's just the way things are.

7 Look at these extracts from the podcast. Complete rules 1–6 with a–f below.

1 We use the *-ing* form in these extracts because …
Having something like that on your travels has to be good.
… what's more embarrassing – the translation or *saying* your mate's mum is 'nice'?

2 We use the *-ing* form in these extracts because …
Good for *scaring* your little brother …
What's wrong with *using* your own voice?

3 We use the *-ing* form in this extract because …
… what's more *embarrassing* …?

4 We use the *-ing* form in these extracts because …
Someone's *following* you – a robber or worse.
… some creep's *considering* robbing me …

5 We use the infinitive with *to* in this extract because …
You can use the app on your phone *to lock* or unlock it from anywhere.

6 We use the *-ing* form and the infinitive with *to* in these extracts because …
You don't think he might be more tempted *to rob* me?
Imagine *walking* home at night …
It's an app that allows you *to speak* in a foreign language you don't know.
… some creep's considering *robbing* me …

a it's part of a continuous tense.

b some *-ing* forms are adjectives.

c we want to use a verb as a subject or object of a sentence. (It's like a noun.)

d we always use an *-ing* form of the verb after a preposition. (It's like a noun.)

e some verbs are always followed by an *-ing* form and others are always followed by an infinitive with *to* – that's just the way it is!

f we want to explain the purpose or reason for something.

(G) Check your ideas on page 92 and do Exercise 1.

8 Decide if the sentences below are correct or incorrect. If there is a mistake, correct it.

1 I should get a new computer because it keeps to crash.

2 They should bring out an app to do my school assignments automatically.

3 To make your own films is much easier with this new software because the user interface is really clear.

4 I saved so much money after buying this gadget that measures how much electricity is being used in the house.

5 I never turn down the heating for to save energy.

6 We're all guilty of to damage the planet in some way.

7 People need to get used to not drive everywhere. They should walk more.

8 I took the laptop back to the shop and luckily they agreed to exchange it.

9 Complete the sentences so they are true for you. Use an *-ing* form or an infinitive with *to*. Then work in pairs and compare your ideas.

1 They should invent a machine …

2 I think … is OK for women, but not for men.

3 I'm hoping … sometime in the future.

4 I keep …

5 I think … is better for you than …

6 I spend most of my weekends …

7 I've arranged … at the weekend.

(G) For further practice, see Exercise 2 on page 93.

SPEAKING

10 Work in groups. Look at each of the gadgets and apps below and decide how you think they work, why people might need them and if they are totally great or total rubbish. You must choose one or the other and you must all agree.

- a set of bicycle handlebars with GPS built in
- a waterless egg boiler
- a T-shirt that records your heart rate and other data
- an app to calculate how long food or drink will take to reach a specific temperature in the fridge or oven
- a pen that allows you to draw in 3D
- a pillow with built-in speakers
- an app that turns your phone into a torch
- a machine to exercise dogs

11 With your group, talk about gadgets or apps that you think are rubbish. Explain why.

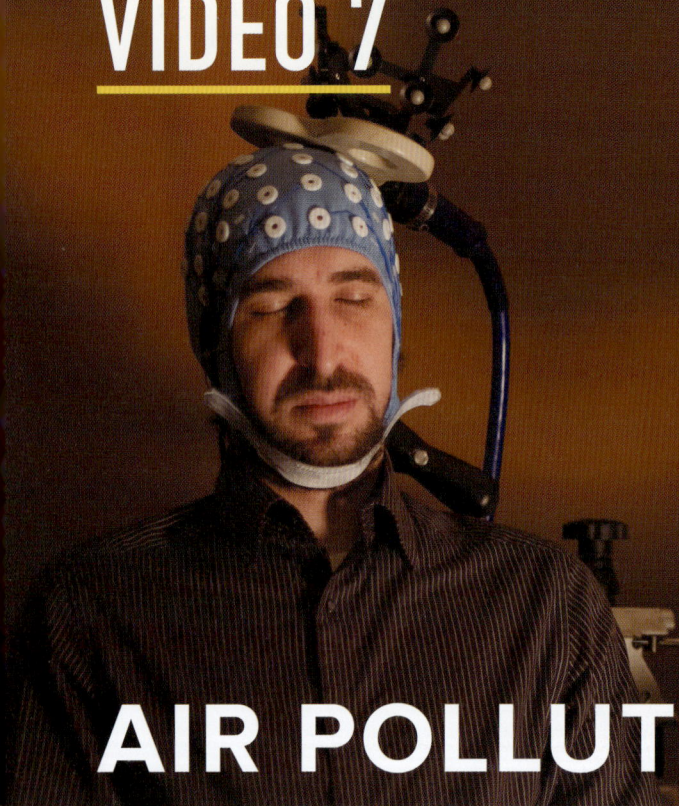

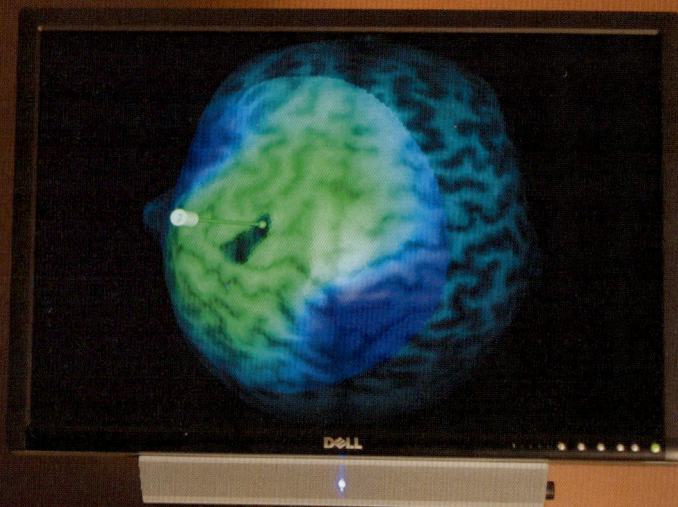

AIR POLLUTION TRACKING

1 Work in pairs. Look at the photo and discuss the questions.

- What do you think the purpose of the experiment is?
- How do you think the experiment works?
- Have you ever taken part in any experiments or research of any kind?

2 Complete the definitions below with these words from the video you are going to watch.

asthma	data	sensor	urban
breathe	volunteer	pollution	GPS

1 If you collect _____ , you gather information that can be analysed.

2 If there are high levels of _____ , then there are lots of dangerous chemicals in the air.

3 If you study the air in cities, you research the _____ atmosphere.

4 When you _____ , you take air into your lungs through your mouth or nose.

5 A _____ tracking system uses satellite technology to help you find your way around.

6 If you suffer from _____ , you have a medical condition that makes it hard to breathe.

7 If you _____ – or if you are a _____ – you offer to work for no money.

8 A piece of equipment that reacts to changes in the physical environment is called a _____ .

3 ◼27 Watch the video and answer the questions. Then work in pairs and compare your ideas.

1 What's the research trying to discover?

2 How is the information collected? Who collects it?

3 What might happen once the findings of the research become available?

4 ◼27 With your partner, decide if the sentences are true (T) or false (F). Then watch the video again and check your answers.

1 Cassandra has two children.

2 Her kids suffer from asthma.

3 The air sensors breathe in air once every minute.

4 The GPS tracking system marks where each sample of air was taken.

5 On roads with lots of trucks and buses, the air is generally unhealthy for everyone.

6 Parents are using air pollution data to help them decide where to send their kids to school.

5 Work in groups. Discuss the questions.

- Do you worry about air pollution – or any other kind of pollution? Why? / Why not?
- Do you know any areas in your town / city that would be red / green if they were analysed?
- Can you think of three things about your environment you would like to gather data about?

UNDERSTANDING FAST SPEECH

6 ◼28 Read and listen to this extract from the video said at natural pace and then slowed down. To help you, groups of words are marked with / and pauses are marked //. Stressed sounds are in CAPITALS.

There's a LOT of HEALTH PROBlems / in my comMUnity // and I'd LIKE to FIND OUT // WHAT's in the AIR // and / WHAT my KIDS are BREAthing ALL THREE of my CHILdren // have ASthma.

7 Now you have a go! Practise saying the extract at natural pace.

REVIEW 7

GRAMMAR

1 Complete the text with one word in each space.

I'm ¹_____ computer programmer and I love my job. ²_____ in IT means I can dress how I want, be as creative as I want ³_____ be and work ⁴_____ hours I feel like working. Sometimes, though, it causes problems. Last month, for example, a friend asked me ⁵_____ help her design a website for her company. Looking back on it, I realise that I ⁶_____'ve said no. Honestly, if I ⁷_____ known how much work it'd be, I would never ⁸_____ agreed to help. I spent night after night ⁹_____ to sort out problems with ¹⁰_____ design – and all for nothing, because I didn't get paid for it. It was basically just a favour!

2 Complete the second sentence so that it has a similar meaning to the first sentence using the word given. Do not change the word given. You must use between two and four words, including the word given.

1 I blame myself for eating too much.
It's my own fault. I _____ so much! **NOT**

2 I only forgot to do it because I was exhausted!
If I _____ tired, I'm sure I would've remembered to do it. **SO**

3 If you text while you're driving, of course you're going to have an accident!
It's not really surprising he had an accident. I mean, he _____ texting while he was driving. **HAVE**

4 I was interested in what he was saying in his talk.
I found what he was saying in his talk _____ . **ABSOLUTELY**

5 It's really hard to find affordable accommodation in the centre of town.
We're faced with _____ somewhere that's both cheap and central! **PROBLEM**

3 Choose the correct option.

1 I *would've / wouldn't have* probably been OK if the flight *had / hadn't* been so bumpy.

2 Thank you so much. I *could / couldn't* have done it if you *had / hadn't* helped me.

3 It's my fault. I *should / shouldn't* probably have updated the software more often.

4 We *shouldn't stop / shouldn't have stopped* for lunch. If we *did / had / hadn't*, we *wouldn't miss / wouldn't have missed* the flight.

5 It's quite easy to play. Basically, you gather resources *for / for to / to* build your own little town.

6 He was caught *to try / trying / try* to take a gun through security.

7 It allows you *experience / experiencing / to experience* motorway driving in extreme conditions without risking your life!

8 It's *amazing / an amazing / the amazing* piece of technology!

9 *Life / The life* for most students currently at *university / a university / the university* is going to be hard in the future.

4 ▶ 68 Listen and write the six sentences you hear.

5 Write a sentence before and after the sentences from Exercise 4 to create short dialogues.

VOCABULARY

6 Match the verbs (1–8) with the collocates (a–h).

1 make   a on a tight bend
2 beat   b your best time
3 wait   c the look of the game
4 run   d to the next level
5 enhance   e a backup copy
6 overtake   f a tyre
7 advance   g on the wrong platform
8 change   h a security scan

7 Decide if these words and phrases are connected to journeys, technology or games.

advance to the next level	set off
built-in sensors	on a mission
beat your best time	interface
run on solar power	ferry
a rough crossing	swipe
gather resources	carriage

8 Complete the sentences. Use the word in brackets to form a word that fits in the space.

1 It's very user-friendly and you can make your own _____ as well. (modify)

2 With the new technology that's available, the _____ are endless. (possible)

3 Have you checked all the _____ ? Something might not be plugged in. (connect)

4 Businesses owned and run by women make a considerable _____ to the national economy. (contribute)

5 Be careful out there. The roads are really _____ . (slip)

6 It's a great app. It sends me a _____ a week before important birthdays. (remind)

9 Complete the text with one word in each space. The first letters are given.

I went sailing last weekend with an old friend of mine. We met at her place, and then walked down to the ¹ha_____ , where she keeps her boat. We set ²sa_____ quite early and the weather was amazing – absolutely ³bo_____ . After an hour or so, though, the sea starting getting ⁴ro_____ and before long we were being hit by these ⁵h_____ waves. Then the storm started and it absolutely ⁶po_____ down. It was really scary. I honestly thought we were going to sink! Then I almost went overboard! I ⁷tr_____ over a rope on the ⁸de_____ and only just managed to grab something to hold onto. I guess it was my own ⁹fa_____ , as I was wearing the wrong shoes, but it was still quite an ¹⁰or_____ and certainly not something I want to go ¹¹th_____ again! It took me quite a while to ¹²ca_____ myself down after that, I can tell you.

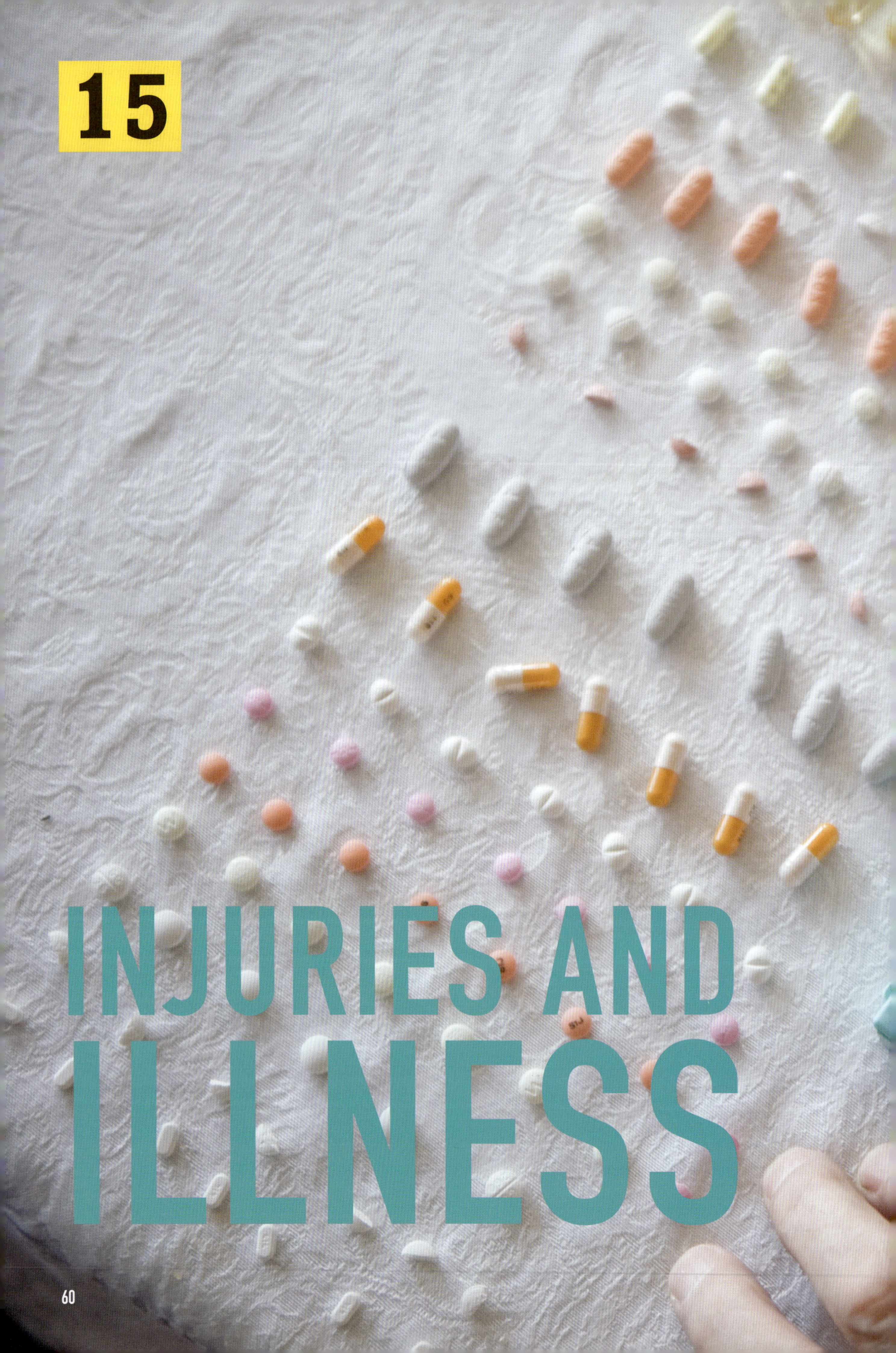

15

INJURIES AND ILLNESS

IN THIS UNIT YOU LEARN HOW TO:

- talk about injuries and illness with a doctor
- discuss health myths and facts
- talk about causes and results
- tell stories about accidents
- report what people said

SPEAKING

1 **Work in groups. Look at the photo and discuss the questions.**

- What do you think the photo shows?
- Do you think it shows a positive or a negative view of health and medicine? Why?
- What kinds of things do you think the pills might be for?
- What different kinds of medication can you buy in a chemist's without a prescription?
- How are the following conditions usually treated?

a broken bone	a rash	a sprain
a nasty cut	flu	an allergy

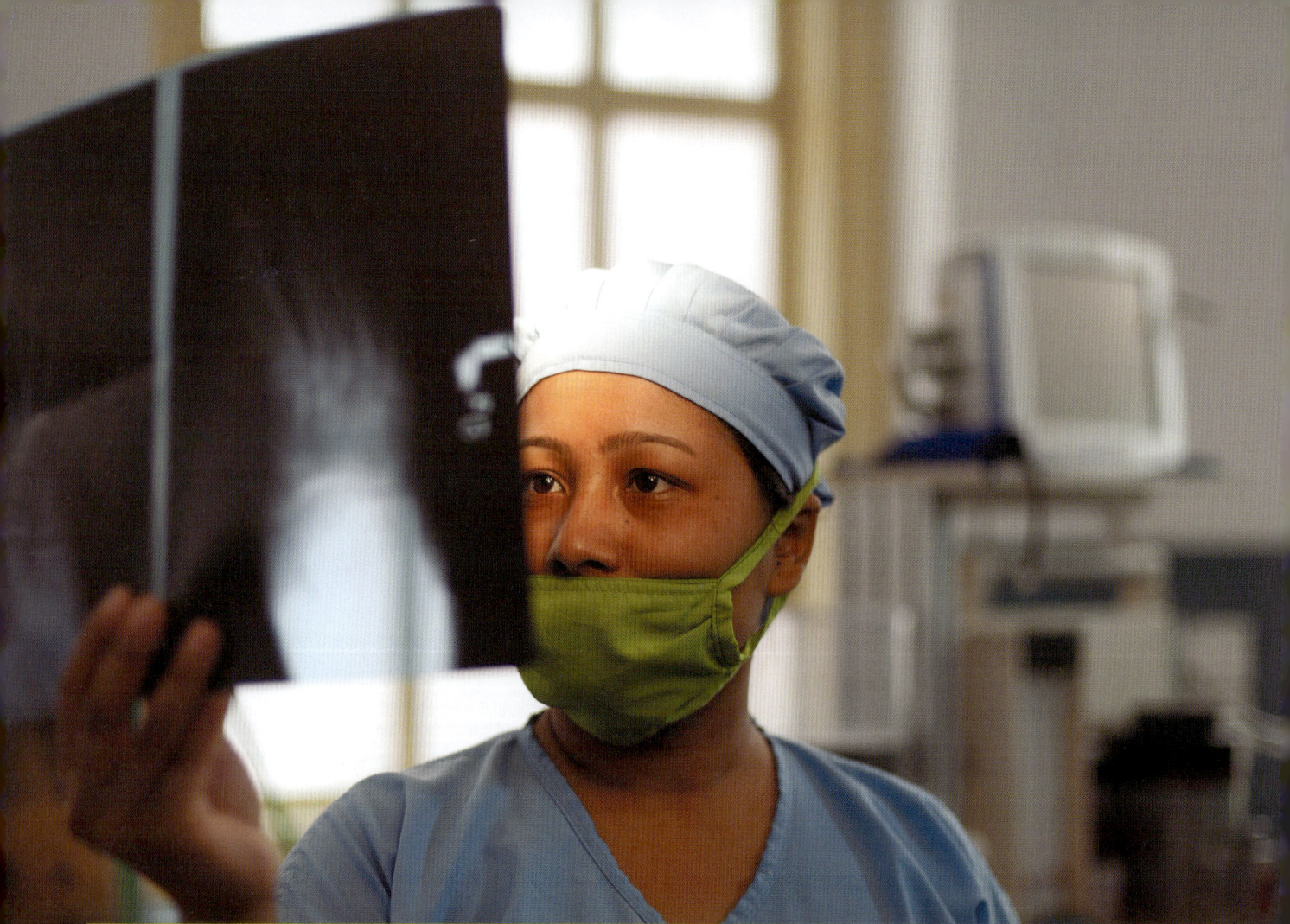

WHAT SEEMS TO BE THE PROBLEM?

VOCABULARY Injuries and illness

1 Match the doctor's comments 1–5 with the patient's replies a–e. Then match the patient's comments 6–10 with the doctor's replies f–j.

1 You've broken your **collarbone**, I'm afraid.

2 Your **throat** is very **sore**, but it doesn't look **infected**.

3 It's quite a **nasty cut**. It'll take a while to **heal**.

4 We can **give you an injection** for the pain. Are you **on** any **medication**?

5 You've got very **high blood pressure**.

a Well, I have been **under a lot of stress** recently.

b Oh no! How long will it take to **mend**?

c Will it need any **stitches**?

d Yes, I take something for **a heart condition** and a **dust allergy.**

e Right. Is there anything that'll make it easier to **swallow**?

6 My **ankle**'s **swollen** and it really **hurts**. I can hardly walk on it.

7 I've developed this **rash** on my skin. It's really red.

8 I felt **dizzy** and fell and hit my head.

9 I've had this **nasty cough** for weeks.

10 I've had a **high temperature** and an **upset stomach**.

f It's **a chest infection**. It should **clear up with antibiotics**.

g I'm afraid there's **a virus going around**. Just rest and drink lots of **fluids**.

h It's probably just **sprained**, but we'll give you some **painkillers** and **do an X-ray** to check.

i Yeah, that's a **nasty bruise**. Did you actually **lose consciousness**?

j It could be **a reaction to** an insect bite. I'll give you some **cream** for it.

2 Work in groups. Take turns to act, draw or explain the words and phrases in bold. Your partners should say the words and phrases.

3 With your group, take turns to tell your partners things which are true about you or people you know using as many of the words in bold in Exercise 1 as you can. You have three minutes each.

LISTENING

4 ▶ **69** You are going to hear two conversations in a hospital. Work in pairs. Look at the questions asked in each conversation and discuss what you think is wrong with the patients. Then listen and check your ideas.

Conversation 1

1 Can you put any weight on it at all?
2 How did you do it?
3 How long will I have to wait for the X-ray?
4 Are you on any medication?
5 Have you ever had any adverse reactions to any painkillers?

Conversation 2

6 What seems to be the problem?
7 How long have you been like this?
8 Any diarrhoea?
9 Has he been able to drink anything?
10 Does it hurt? And here?

5 ▶ **69** Listen again. Note down the answers to the questions.

6 Work in pairs. Look at Track 69 on page 107 and practise reading the conversations.

GRAMMAR

> ### Adverbs
> We can use adverbs to add information to verbs and show the way things happen, how frequently they happen or when they happen. We also use adverbs to show our opinion or attitude about something we're saying.

7 Complete the sentences from the conversations with these adverbs.

quite	badly	hardly	lately	hard
first	hopefully	fast	long	really

1 It might just be _____ sprained.
2 Have you been waiting _____ ?
3 We've been a bit short of staff _____ .
4 _____ , it won't be more than half an hour.
5 He's _____ slept.
6 His heart was beating _____ _____ .
7 He _____ said he felt a bit sick yesterday.
8 I'm going to press _____ _____ .

8 Look at the sentences in Exercise 7 again. Then work in pairs and decide if the statements below are true (T) or false (F).

1 Adverbs are always based on adjectives and end in -ly.
2 Adjectives can sometimes have two adverb forms.
3 Any adverb can be placed: at the beginning or end of a sentence, and before a verb or after a verb.

G Check your ideas on page 93 and do Exercise 1.

9 Correct the mistakes with the adverbs in these sentences.

1 I have been under a lot of stress because I've been working so hardly.
2 Have you had any of these symptoms previous?
3 You shouldn't go to bed so lately. You need to get some rest.
4 Open your mouth widely and say 'ahhh'.
5 It was my fault it happened. I was incredible stupid.
6 Never should you leave pills where children can reach them easy.
7 Can you just say it again slowlier, please?
8 It doesn't hurt. I can feel it hardly.

DEVELOPING CONVERSATIONS

> ### Short questions with *any*
> We often shorten questions with *any*, especially when they follow other related questions.
>
> Have you ever had **any** adverse reactions to any painkillers? → **Any** adverse reactions to painkillers?
>
> Do you have **any** questions? → **Any** questions?

10 Match the two parts of the questions.

1	Any pain	a	for the weekend?
2	Any symptoms	b	you want to know?
3	Any idea	c	apart from the cough?
4	Any questions	d	what it is, doctor?
5	Anything else	e	want to help me?
6	Anyone	f	when I press here?
7	Any plans	g	from Frank recently?
8	Any news	h	before you go?

11 Write your own endings for the first halves of the questions 1–8 in Exercise 10. Then work in pairs. Practise asking and answering the questions.

A: *Any pain when you stand on it?*
B: *A little.*

CONVERSATION PRACTICE

12 Work in pairs. You are going to roleplay a conversation between a patient and a doctor. First decide together on a medical problem.

Student A: you are the patient. Think of details of your problem and plan what questions to ask the doctor.

Student B: you are the doctor. Decide what advice to give.

13 Now roleplay the conversation. Use as much new language from this lesson as possible.

🎥 29 To watch the video and do the activities, see the DVD ROM.

IT'S A BIT OF A MYTH

READING

1 Work in pairs. Look at the following claims and discuss if you think they are true. Explain your ideas.

1 You can catch a cold if you go out with wet hair.
2 Antibiotics can cure a cold.
3 Eating chocolate can cause acne.
4 Cracking the joints in your fingers can cause arthritis.
5 Having less cholesterol in your diet prevents heart attacks.
6 Swallowing chewing gum is bad for you.
7 Coffee is a drug.

2 Read the article from a health website opposite. Decide if the claims in Exercise 1 are true or if they are myths, according to the writer. Why?

3 Work in groups. Without looking at the article, see if you can remember:

1 what mothers often tell their children.
2 the best way to avoid catching a cold.
3 when you may need antibiotics.
4 the best way to deal with a cold.
5 what makes acne worse.
6 what other factors can cause heart attacks.
7 what people think happens when they eat chewing gum.
8 what can happen when people give up coffee.

4 Look at the article again. Did you remember the exact words?

5 Work in groups. Discuss the questions.

- Was there anything in the article that surprised you?
- Is there anything in the article you disagree with? Why?
- Do you know any other claims about health issues? Do you think they are myths or facts?
- Do you ever check symptoms or find out about health issues on the Internet? If you do, which sites do you use? If you don't, why not?
- Have there been any news stories about health issues recently? What do you think about them?

6 Look at the phrases in bold in the article. Notice the patterns connected to each verb. Now complete the sentences below with the verbs in bold.

1 Sitting too close to the television can _____ to problems with your eyes.
2 Children who watch a lot of TV spend too much time sitting, which _____ their health suffers.
3 Apparently, watching a lot of TV can _____ people to become depressed.
4 Young children will get better grades later at school if you _____ them watch videos of great artists and classical composers.

5 Increases in violent crime are _____ by the increased violence shown on TV.
6 Watching TV late at night _____ it difficult to get to sleep.

7 Work in groups. Which of the sentences in Exercise 6 do you think are myths? Why?

8 Write four sentences like those in Exercise 6 about health fears / benefits connected to the things below. They may be facts or myths! Then share your sentences in groups. Try to decide which are facts and which are myths. Explain your ideas.

mobile phones	vitamins
computer games	sugar

UNDERSTANDING VOCABULARY

Word endings and word class

The endings of words often show their word class. For example:

- *-ious* / *-ic* / *-able* / *-ful* / *-less* / *-ive* / *-al* indicate adjectives
- *-ion* / *-ment* / *-ness* / *-ance* / *-ence* / *-ist* indicate nouns
- *-ise* / *-en* indicate verbs
- *-ly* indicates adverbs (but not always!)

You can build your vocabulary by learning connected word forms of new items you meet.

9 Work in pairs and look at these words from this unit. Think of other words you can make from these words and say if each is an adjective, a noun, a verb or an adverb. Use a dictionary to help you.

benefit	injection	prevent	stimulant
consciousness	nutritional	painful	treatment

10 Choose the correct option.

1 A viral *infectious* / *infection* can't be treated with antibiotics.
2 I know several people who are *allergic* / *allergy* to nuts.
3 I'm often quite *irritable* / *irritation* when I wake up in the morning.
4 I'm sure most diseases will be *cure* / *curable* by the end of this century.
5 I do *regular* / *regularly* exercise.
6 Most *medical* / *medicine* conditions are the result of poor diet.
7 They need to *modernise* / *modern* our health service.
8 All drugs are *addictive* / *addiction*.

11 Work in pairs. Read out the sentences you agree with from Exercise 10 and explain why.

FACT OR MYTH?

1 It's difficult to ignore your mother when she tells you to 'wrap up warm' or 'dry your hair or you'll get a cold' – but colds **are not caused by the cold**: they **are caused by viruses**! Walking around with wet hair or a T-shirt in winter may look silly, and will **make you feel cold**, but you will only get a cold if you come into contact with an infected person. The best way to avoid viruses like these is to wash your hands regularly when there's a bug going around.

2 Despite the huge medical advances that have been made over the last century, the common cold is still incurable and medicine does little for the symptoms either. Antibiotics won't help as your cold **is caused by one of over 200 viruses**. The only time you may need them is if you develop a throat or ear infection. Otherwise, go to bed and drink lots of fluids and wait till you get better.

3 Acne is a condition **that causes the skin to produce** too much oil. However, research has failed to find any connection between eating fatty foods and acne – although too much fat in your diet might be bad in other ways. Incidentally, washing too much can **make the condition worse**. It's best just to wash gently twice a day and don't rub the skin too hard.

4 Arthritis affects all kinds of people, including young children who have never started cracking their fingers. Suffering from a **viral infection may lead to developing the condition**, as might jobs which involve an overuse of your joints, but doctors are still not sure of the real cause.

5 You can buy foods that are advertised as being low in cholesterol or able to reduce how much you have, so you might think cholesterol is an entirely bad thing. You'd be wrong. Cholesterol is essential for life and is produced naturally by the body. The body also adjusts how much it produces based on what you eat. If you eat food containing a lot of cholesterol, your body simply produces less in order to balance its two sources. This **means it's difficult** to reduce cholesterol in the body through diet. Some doctors have even questioned if there is any link between cholesterol levels and heart disease. They point to factors such as lack of exercise, smoking, stress and high blood pressure that are far more likely **to lead to heart attacks**.

6 Don't worry. Stories that chewing gum will stay in your stomach forever or block your insides have no basis in fact. However, it has no nutritional value **which means you won't get any benefits** from eating it.

7 The caffeine in coffee is a stimulant that makes your body speed up: your heart rate increases and it wakes you up. You may see these things as benefits, but caffeine also has a number of negative side effects. It's addictive. People who suddenly stop drinking coffee may suffer from headaches or be irritable and restless. Caffeine has also been linked to other problems, but, like most things, coffee is fine if you don't drink too much.

Remember this is for information only. If you have any worries about your health, you should always consult your doctor.

'I ONLY HAVE ONE CUP OF COFFEE A DAY'

Comments 14 | Add a comment | Share

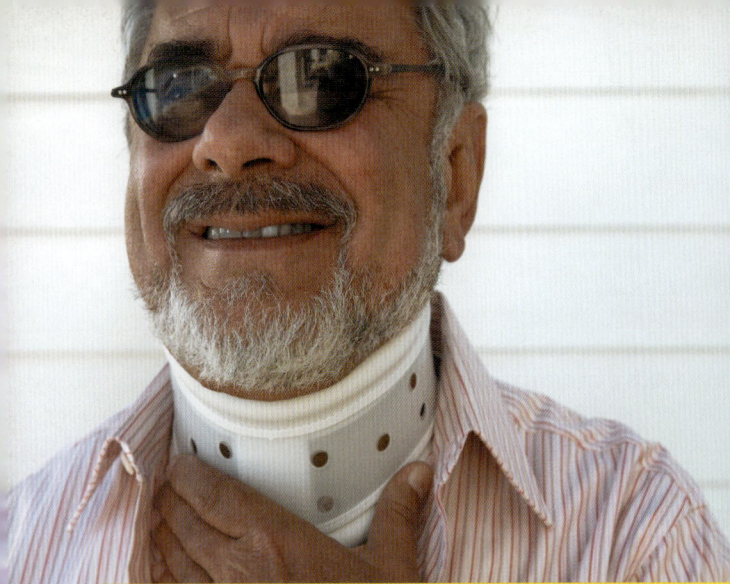

ACCIDENTS AND INJURIES

SPEAKING

1 Look at eight different places where accidents often happen. Rank them from 1 (= most dangerous) to 8 (= least dangerous). Then work in pairs and compare your lists.

the kitchen	the bathroom
the countryside	the living room
the garden	the gym
the park	the roads near your home

VOCABULARY Accidents and health problems

2 Choose the correct option.

1 I was grilling some meat and I caught my hand on the grill and *burned* / *bruised* it quite badly.

2 I was jogging and I *tripped* / *slipped* over a rock and hurt my knee really badly.

3 I was out riding and the horse got scared by a bang and I *fell off* / *fell down* the horse and broke my collarbone.

4 I was walking down the street and this dog suddenly attacked me and *bit* / *stung* me on the leg.

5 I was cycling and a car drove in front of me. I *crashed into* / *fell into* the side and sprained my wrist.

6 I had some food at a street market and I think I got food *infection* / *poisoning* from there. It was awful.

7 I spent the whole day on the beach and ended up with terrible *suntan* / *sunburn*.

8 It was really hot on the underground and I felt dizzy and then just *fainted* / *fell down*.

9 I broke my arm when I *tripped* / *slipped* on some ice.

10 This bee *stung* / *bit* me on the arm and my whole arm swelled up.

3 Work in groups. Can you think of:

1 two other things you can trip over, apart from a rock?

2 two parts of the body that often get bruised? Say how.

3 two other things you can fall off, apart from a horse?

4 two other things that can bite you, apart from dogs?

5 two kinds of food you could get food poisoning from?

6 two other reasons why people sometimes faint?

7 two other things you can slip on, apart from ice?

8 two other things that can sting you, apart from a bee?

LISTENING

4 ▶ 70 Listen to Anna talking to her colleague Dan about his holiday. Answer the questions.

1 What kind of holiday was it?

2 How did the accident happen?

3 What did they think was wrong with James?

4 How did they get him to a hospital?

5 What did the doctors tell him?

5 ▶ 70 Work in pairs. Put the events from the story into the correct order. Listen again and check your answers.

a He had quite a few cuts and bruises.

b It spoilt his holiday.

c James went off the road into some bushes and fell off.

d He had to have a few stitches in the cuts.

e She took him to hospital, which was really kind of her.

f We were going back to the hotel down a steep road.

g He found out his bike frame was broken.

h A woman came past in her car a minute or two later.

6 Work in pairs. Discuss the questions.

• Do you like cycling? Have you ever been on a cycling holiday? When? Where?

• When was the last time someone was very kind to you? What did they do?

• When was the last time you were very kind to someone else? What did you do?

• Did Dan's story about James remind you of any other stories you have heard?

GRAMMAR

Reported speech

When we tell people about things that happened to us, we often report things using *said / told me (that)* + clause. We also report questions using *ask me / us* + clause.

7 Look at these sentences from the conversation. Answer the questions below.

a *He **kept asking us** where he **was** and what **had happened**.*

b *He even **asked** if we**'d met** somewhere before!*

c *The woman driving **said** she**'d take** James to the nearest hospital.*

d *He **kept saying** he**'d be** OK.*

e *They rang and **told me** they**'d given** James an X-ray and there **was** nothing broken.*

f *They **said** he **needed** to stay there a bit longer, as he **was waiting** to have a few stitches in the cuts.*

g *He **said** he**'s going to** have to buy a new bike now.*

1 Can you name the structures in bold?

2 What do you think the people actually said in each case?

3 When we report what people said, what often happens to tenses and words like *will* and *can*?

4 What's different about sentence g)? Why is it different?

5 Which sentences report questions? How do reported questions differ from direct questions?

G Check your ideas on page 94 and do Exercise 1.

8 Complete the sentences with the correct past form of the verbs. Then decide in which of the sentences the present form would also be possible.

1 The doctor told me I _____ a chest infection and _____ me some antibiotics. It cleared up after a week. (have, give)

2 The doctor said he _____ too much and he _____ to go on a diet, but he refused. (eat, need)

3 The doctors said she _____ some problems in the future, but she _____ incredibly lucky to survive the crash. (have, be)

4 The doctor told me the injection _____ , but it _____ really painful! (not / hurt, be)

5 They said the surgeon _____ all she _____ to keep him alive. (do, can)

6 She told me they _____ several tests already, but they still didn't know what _____ the problem, so they had to do more. (do, cause)

7 They asked me how it _____ and whether or not it ever _____ me any pain. (happen, cause)

8 He asked if I _____ his phone conversation and if I _____ more or less what it meant. (hear, understand)

9 Work in pairs. Take turns to ask each other *So what did the doctor say?* Report something different each time.

A: *So what did the doctor say?*

B: *She said I'm quite unfit and I need to do more exercise. So what did the doctor say?*

A: *He asked if I smoke and then told me I need to cut down.*

G For further practice, see Exercise 2 on page 94.

SPEAKING

10 Work in pairs and choose one of these tasks.

a Work in pairs. Talk about a time when you had an accident or were ill. Describe what happened. Use reported speech and vocabulary from this lesson.

b Look at the photos on these pages. Choose one and imagine you are the person in it. Decide how to describe your accident / injury. Add extra details about what happened before and after. Then tell your partner your story.

- talk about types and sources of news
- comment on the news
- use reporting verbs to report news
- describe famous people and events
- discuss issues around fame

SPEAKING

1   Look at the photo and imagine what the news story is. Think about these questions.

- Who is the man being interviewed?
- What did he do or what happened to him?
- Where is he now?
- What will happen next?

Then work in pairs and tell each other your stories.

2   Work in groups. Tell each other which of the types of news below you are most interested in and say where you get your news from. Who is most similar to you in the group?

crime and justice	foreign affairs
business and economics	national politics
celebrities and gossip	reviews and entertainment
weather	funny news stories
technology	sport

NEWS AND EVENTS

IN THE HEADLINES

VOCABULARY News

1 Work in pairs. Match each group of words below to the type of news on page 69 they are connected to.

1 _____
have an affair
be photographed
split up
_____

2 _____
expand
go bankrupt
be taken over
_____

3 _____
be injured
be beaten
sign a player
_____

4 _____
resign
be elected
introduce a policy
_____

5 _____
be found guilty
be stabbed
investigate
_____

6 _____
hold a summit
call a ceasefire
negotiate
_____

2 Put these nouns in the correct group (1–6) in Exercise 1.

share price	film premiere	deputy mayor
victim	peace agreement	new season

3 Work in groups. Give an example of recent news for each type of news in Exercise 1. Try to use at least one word from each group of words.

LISTENING

4 ▶ **71** Listen to five short conversations about news stories. Match each conversation (1–5) to one of the following. There is one that you do not need.

a a football player

b a politician

c a celebrity

d a violent crime

e a factory

f a law firm

5 ▶ **71** Listen again and note down which of the words from Exercises 1 and 2 were used in each conversation. Then work in pairs and summarise each news story.

6 Work with a new partner. Look at Track 71 on page 108. Choose the two conversations you think are most interesting. Read them out loud and continue each conversation for as long as you can by adding your own ideas and comments.

GRAMMAR

Reporting verbs

When we report a conversation, we sometimes use different verbs to introduce what was said, such as *announce* or *claim*. Sometimes we use verbs such as *promise* or *apologise* to summarise what was said rather than repeat the exact words. These verbs are often followed by different patterns.

7 Look at these sentences from the conversations. Put them into three groups (1–3) of reporting verbs that follow the same pattern.

a *She's just **announced** they're splitting up.*

b *They even **promised** to expand last year.*

c *He's been **accused** of doing all kinds of things.*

d *Not that he's **admitted** to doing anything.*

e *The new management **claim** it's too expensive to run.*

f *He just **apologised** for 'causing the government difficulties'.*

g *No-one **offered** to help the victim.*

h *He's **refused** to play in any friendly matches.*

G Check your ideas on page 95 and do Exercise 1.

8 Work in pairs. Think of an example from the news where a person or organisation:

1 was accused of something.

2 had to apologise for something.

3 announced something important.

4 refused to do something.

5 gave a warning.

6 made an offer.

G For further practice, see Exercise 2 on page 95.

DEVELOPING CONVERSATIONS

Introducing and commenting on news

Conversations about the news often have common features. You can start the conversation using this common pattern or similar questions:

Did you see that thing on the Times website **about** the steel plant clos**ing** down?

If you know the story you can comment using one of these patterns:

Yeah, **it's** shocking, **isn't it**?

I know, **it's** bad news, **isn't it**?

You can give details about the story starting with *apparently*. It shows you are reporting what you heard or read.

Apparently, he took illegal payments …

9 Complete the questions about news by putting the words in brackets into the correct order.

1 Have you seen that thing _____ (player / on / about / Twitter / that / tennis), James Jenkins?

2 Have you seen that video _____ (on / of / the / prime / YouTube / dance / minister / trying / to) to hip-hop?

3 Did you see that thing _____ (TV / about / on / them / new / a / airport / building)?

4 Did you see that thing _____ (the / news / on / about / the / here / murder / near) last night?

5 Did you see that thing _____ (the / website / arrested / Times / about / Shaynee Wilson / getting / on)?

10 Match the responses (a–e) to the questions (1–5) in Exercise 9.

a Yeah, it's good news, isn't it? Apparently, it's going to create 1,000 jobs.

b Yeah, it's sad, isn't it? The media are obsessed with that woman.

c Yeah, it's awful, isn't it? Apparently, the victim was quite young.

d Yeah, it's so funny, isn't it? Apparently, it was from before he went into politics, though.

e Yeah, what an idiot. Apparently, it's been retweeted a million times already.

PRONUNCIATION

11 ▶ **72** Listen and check your answers to Exercise 10. Notice how the intonation falls on *it's X, isn't it?* to show we are agreeing.

12 Work in pairs and practise reading out the exchanges, paying attention to the falling intonation on the *it's X, isn't it?* patterns.

13 With your partner, take turns saying the sentences below. Respond with an *it's X, isn't it?* comment.

1 Did you hear about Jay and Selma splitting up?

2 Did you hear about John getting food poisoning from his own cooking?

3 Did you read about Angelina booking a special hotel room for her dog?

4 Did you see that the ceasefire has ended already?

5 Did you see that thing in the paper about that woman who paid $5,000 for that dress?

6 Did you hear that Jay and Selma are back together?

CONVERSATION PRACTICE

14 Think of two news stories you have read or heard about recently. Write one question for each story, using patterns like those in Exercise 9.

15 Work in groups. Discuss the stories. Start your conversations with your questions from Exercise 14.

🎥 30 To watch the video and do the activities, see the DVD ROM.

I'VE NEVER HEARD OF HIM

SPEAKING

1 Work in groups. Do you know who the people in the photos are? Use some of the language below.

- I haven't got a clue!
- He looks really familiar, but I can't remember who he is.
- Isn't he that American politician? What's his name?
- I'm fairly sure that's ...

VOCABULARY
Explaining who people are

2 The sentences below describe some of the people in the photos. Complete the sentences with these words. Then work in pairs and match them to the photos.

activist	artist
athlete	politician
doctor	founder
mathematician	scientist

1 Marie Curie was a Polish _____ who **studied radiation and discovered** the radioactive substance polonium.

2 Nelson Mandela was a civil rights _____ who **campaigned for the rights of** black people in South Africa. He became the country's first black president in 1994.

3 Takako Doi was perhaps the most important female _____ Japan has ever had. She was leader of the Socialist Party and **was responsible for** bringing more women into politics.

4 Kemal Atatürk **led the liberation struggle in** Turkey and became **a national hero**. He was then the _____ of the republic.

5 Martina Navratilova is a Czech / American **former** tennis player. **She's seen by some as the greatest** female _____ **of all time**. She **completely dominated the sport** for many years.

6 Euclid was a Greek _____ who **is considered to be the father of** geometry. He was **a genius** and **way ahead of his time**.

7 Pedro Alonso is a Spanish _____ . He led a team which **developed a vaccine against** malaria.

8 Salvador Dali was a Spanish Catalan _____ whose **most famous work** is probably 'The Persistence of Memory'.

3 With your partner, check you understand the phrases in bold in Exercise 2. Then use as many of the phrases as you can to talk about other famous people – living or dead.

LISTENING

4 ▶ 73 Listen to three conversations about famous people. Answer the questions for each conversation.

1 Why do they start talking about Garibaldi / Comenius / Eddy Merckx / Magritte?

2 What is each person famous for?

3 Where is each person from?

4 What else do you learn about each one?

5 Work in pairs. Can you think of:

1 a statue of a famous person?

2 someone who is seen as a national hero?

3 someone who was way ahead of their time?

4 a place that is named after a famous person?

5 a place that is decorated with memorabilia?

GRAMMAR
Defining relative clauses

6 Underline the relative clauses in these sentences. The first one has been done for you. Then complete the rules in the Grammar box below.

a It's a European Union scheme <u>which provides grants to teachers</u>.

b He was a Czech writer who wrote about education.

c When I went to Belgium I visited the metro station where they have Eddy Merckx's bike.

d Michael Jordan was an athlete whose strength and skill inspired millions around the world.

e They left South Africa during the time that Mandela was in prison.

We use relative clauses to add information after nouns. Clauses begin with different relative pronouns depending on the noun we are adding information to or on the information that follows.

• To add information about people, use a clause beginning with *that* or [1]_____ .

• To add information about things, use a clause beginning with *that* or [2]_____ .

• To add information about times, use a clause beginning with *when* or [3]_____ .

• To add information about possessions, use a clause beginning with [4]_____ .

• To add information about places, use a clause beginning with [5]_____ .

G Check your ideas on page 95 and do Exercise 1.

7 Cross out the word or words that are *not* correct.

1 He was a military leader in the nineteenth century *who / that / which* helped unify Italy.

2 It's a European Union scheme *that / who / which* provides grants to teachers.

3 It's *who / when / where* they have Rembrandt's most famous paintings.

4 He set up a charity *that / which / where* has helped thousands of poor children.

5 He's a composer *who / that / whose* most famous work is probably *The Rite of Spring*.

6 At the time *that / who / when* he was writing, his ideas were very radical.

7 It's supposed to be the house *when / where / that* Shakespeare was born.

8 She was a writer *whose / who / which* ideas were very influential.

8 Write down a name for each of the following that you think other students may not know.

1 a writer, artist or musician

2 a scientist or inventor

3 an athlete or sportsman / sportswoman

4 a politician or person from history

5 two places of historical importance

9 Work in groups. Take turns to test each other. Ask *Do you know who X is? / Do you know why X is important?* See who has the best general knowledge and can answer the most questions. When answering or explaining, use relative clauses.

A: *Do you know who Tim Berners-Lee is?*

B: *No, sorry. I haven't got a clue.*

C: *He's the guy who invented the World Wide Web. He's British, I think.*

B: *Oh, OK. Do you know why Robben Island is important?*

A: *Yeah. It's where Nelson Mandela spent all those years in prison.*

G For further practice, see Exercise 2 on page 96.

THE FAME GAME

READING

1 Read the introduction of the article below. Then work in pairs and discuss the questions.

- Why do you think so many people want to be famous?
- What kind of problems might be caused by the desire for fame and money?
- What do you think is the best way to become famous?
- Can you think of any bad ways of becoming famous?
- Do you know about any celebrities who have found fame hard to cope with?
- Which six different ways of becoming rich and famous do you expect the article to mention?

2 Read the rest of the article. In which section were the following mentioned?

a a popular talent show

b retired people

c an act of great generosity

d an act of great bravery

e advertising on a website

f physical attraction

3 Work in pairs. Discuss why the people and things below were mentioned. Check your ideas by looking at the article again if you need to.

1 the gossip magazines	6 Paris Hilton
2 karaoke	7 Golda Bechal
3 Kurt Nilsen	8 Kuldeep Singh
4 Howard Davies-Carr	9 The Zimmers
5 YouTube	10 The Who

4 Work in groups. Can you think of any other people who have become famous in the six ways mentioned in the article? Say as much about them as you can.

SEEKING FAME & FORTUNE

In a recent survey, over 80% of 18-to-25-year-olds said getting rich was their first or second most important life goal, whilst 51% said the same about becoming famous.

Of course, being a celebrity can be problematic. We have all seen stories about stars turning to drink or drugs as they find themselves unable to cope with the emotional stress of life in the public eye. However, this doesn't seem to discourage anyone. The main problem for many seems to be how to actually become rich and famous – especially if you have no real talent! Given this, here's our six-point guide on how to go about it.

1 Date someone who's already famous

Obviously, finding a famous partner is easier said than done. However, anyone who can manage to catch the eye of a top footballer or movie star can expect to find themselves on the front page of the gossip magazines before too long. This might then be enough to get a TV or advertising company interested and you can end up becoming a star yourself.

2 Go on a reality TV show

The kind of out-of-tune singing that was once reserved for the privacy of a karaoke room has now become prime-time Saturday night TV – and shows such as *The X Factor* and *Pop Idol* have brought instant fame and fortune to hundreds around the world. Take Norwegian Kurt Nilsen, for example. His versions of well-known songs were so popular that he was able to give up his job as a plumber! He then went on to win *World Idol* and became a huge star in his native country. If you can sing, you could follow in Kurt's footsteps. If this option isn't available to you, then why not just try to appear on any of the reality TV shows which require no talent at all from their contestants?

3 Go viral

Charlie bit my finger

The Internet has given many their fifteen minutes of fame. You get a message from a friend containing a link to an online video, a blog or a new site. You have a look, forward the link, and before long, things start getting out of control and a million people have seen it!

And, of course, the more views a video gets, the more money can be made from it. A few years ago, Howard Davies-Carr uploaded a short film of his two sons sitting side by side in a chair. Entitled *Charlie bit my finger*, nothing much happens in it – apart from a finger being bitten. However, the clip is now the fourth most-watched film ever on YouTube and the family has earned hundreds of thousands of pounds from advertising.

5 Complete the sentences with the correct form of these words from the article. Then underline the words that go with them in each sentence.

will	option	footsteps	control	barrier

1 We would love to buy a house and move in together, but on our wages that _____ isn't available to us.

2 My dad wants me to follow in his _____ and join the army, but it's just not what I want to do with my life.

3 Physical disability is no _____ to a successful career.

4 My spending got out of _____ . If you ask me, it's the bank's fault for lending me so much money.

5 My aunt left me a house in her _____ .

save	repay	forward	come into	catch

6 You _____ my life! How can I ever thank you enough? I would've died if you hadn't rescued me.

7 Could you _____ the email from Head Office to me?

8 There were some really good-looking guys at the party, but one in particular _____ my eye.

9 Thanks again for everything you did for us. I hope that one day we can _____ your kindness. All the best, Omar

10 She _____ a lot of money when her father died.

6 Work in pairs. Use three of the underlined groups of words from Exercise 5 to say something about your life.

I'd like to follow in my father's footsteps and become a surgeon.

SPEAKING

7 Work in groups. Discuss what you think each quotation about fame means. How far do you agree with each one? Explain why.

'Fame means millions of people have the wrong idea of who you are.'

'Wealth is like sea-water; the more we drink, the thirstier we become; and the same is true of fame.'

'To people who want to be rich and famous, I'd say get rich first and see if that doesn't cover it.'

'Fame is the thirst of youth.'

'Fame is a constant effort.'

'Fame usually comes to those who are thinking about something else.'

'The longer a man's fame is likely to last, the longer it will be in coming.'

'The day will come when everyone will be famous for fifteen minutes.'

8 Work with another group. Which of the eight quotations do you think is the best? Why?

4 Inherit a fortune

Obviously, if you want to come into a lot of money when one of your loved ones dies, it helps if you have incredibly rich parents – like Paris Hilton's. Alternatively, you just need to be lucky when choosing your friends, like Chinese restaurant owners Kim Sing and Bee Lian Man were. They befriended an elderly widow, Golda Bechal, who then repaid their kindness by leaving the couple £10 million in her will when she died.

5 Become a hero

Kuldeep Singh

One good way of getting yourself in the papers is to save someone's life or catch a wanted criminal. Kuldeep Singh, for instance, became a national hero in India when he removed a bomb from a bus he was driving in Delhi. Mr Singh, who was injured when the bomb later exploded, was widely praised for his courage.

6 Don't give up!

The Zimmers

Age is no barrier to becoming famous either, as plenty of old-age pensioners have proved. The Zimmers are among recent examples: a group of around 40 British pensioners put together by a documentary film maker who was interested in the experiences of the elderly, the band's first singer was 90 when he joined and the oldest member was 101! They had a hit with a cover version of The Who's *My Generation* and went on to appear on TV and travel to America.

VIDEO 8

BEE THERAPY

1 Work in pairs. Discuss the questions.

- How much do you know about bees?
- How do you feel about bees? Why?
- Have you – or anyone you know – ever been stung by a bee? When? What happened?
- Why are bees important to humans?
- What do you think is happening in the photo?
- Read the definitions below. How do you think the words in bold might be connected to bees?

Acupuncture is a traditional way of treating pain. It involves placing needles into particular points on the body.

Histamines are chemicals that are released in the body as part of an allergic reaction. They cause typical allergy symptoms like swelling and itching.

Multiple sclerosis (MS) is a disease that slowly attacks the nerves in the body. Symptoms include a feeling of small sharp points pushing into the skin or a stinging sensation (sometimes called a tingling sensation) as well as a loss of feeling (often called numbness).

When part of your body is under attack, **white blood cells** quickly move to that area to help destroy the harmful substances and prevent illness.

2 ▶ 31 Watch the first part of the video (0.00–1.47). Find out how each of the words in bold in Exercise 1 is connected to bees.

3 ▶ 31 Work in pairs. Discuss why the numbers and things below were mentioned. Watch the first part again and check your ideas.

1	dozens of times	5	6,000
2	six months	6	600
3	twelve years	7	five years
4	200	8	one hour

4 ▶ 31 Watch the second part of the video (1.48–3.46). Are the sentences true (T) or false (F)?

1 To begin with, Mr Chen had his doubts about bee sting therapy.

2 His wife developed a mild form of arthritis.

3 Western medicine didn't really help her.

4 After starting bee sting therapy, it took a very long time for her condition to improve.

5 Bee sting therapy has cured Sho Wan Chen's multiple sclerosis.

6 Most western doctors would disagree with her explanation for the change in her condition.

7 There hasn't yet been enough research to prove that bee sting therapy really works.

8 Sho Wan Chen feels better than she has done for at least a year.

5 Work in groups. Discuss the questions.

- What do you think of bee sting therapy?
- Do you think it's OK to use animals to help find cures for human diseases? Why? / Why not?
- Do you know anyone who's tried acupuncture or other alternative therapies? Why? Did it help?

UNDERSTANDING FAST SPEECH

6 ▶ 32 Read and listen to this extract from the video said at natural pace and then slowed down. To help you, groups of words are marked with / and pauses are marked //. Stressed sounds are in CAPITALS.

EVery WEEK / MISter CHEN / and his aSISStants / TREAT TWO HUNdred PAtients / and SAcrifice SIX THOUsand HOney BEES // The reSULTS / he SAYS / can be asTOUNding

7 Now you have a go! Practise saying the extract at natural pace.

REVIEW 8

1 Complete the text with one word in each space.

A few years ago, the company ¹_____ I was working for officially ²_____ that they ³_____ launching this new scheme that ⁴_____ provide us all with excellent health insurance. My employers ⁵_____ to pay us all sick pay and to cover most medical bills. All we had to do was go for a quick check-up with the doctor. Sounds great, right? Well, I went the ⁶_____ week and got a bit of a shock. The doctor ⁷_____ asking me endless personal questions – you know, like ⁸_____ I was married, ⁹_____ I didn't have any kids yet, and so on. I couldn't believe it! The next thing I knew, the company sent me an email apologising ¹⁰_____ bringing me bad news, and saying I didn't qualify. Incredible! I briefly considered complaining ¹¹_____ the experience to someone, but my dad warned me ¹²_____ to, so I didn't.

2 Complete the second sentence so that it has a similar meaning to the first sentence using the word given. Do not change the word given. You must use between two and five words, including the word given.

1 I offered to pay, but he refused to even listen!
He absolutely _____ , even though I offered myself. **PAYING**

2 After hours of questioning, he finally told them he'd cheated in the exam.
In the end, after hours of questioning, he _____ in the exam. **TO**

3 I've always wanted to go to Abbey Road. The Beatles recorded there.
I've always wanted to go to Abbey Road, _____ The Beatles recorded. **PLACE**

4 I can't understand you. Can you speak a bit more slowly?
Sorry, but I can't follow you. You're speaking a bit _____ for me. **TOO**

5 He seemed sure everything was going to be fine.
He kept saying _____ OK. **WOULD**

3 Choose all the correct options.

1 That's the hospital *that / which / where* I had my operation in a few years ago.

2 We met during the time *when / which / that* I was working in the Munich office.

3 He was a military leader *who / that / which* inspired great loyalty in his men.

4 He said he *was going to / is going to / would* do it sometime later in the year.

5 He *suggested / complained / refused* to consider my suggestion.

6 He kept asking what *had happened / was happening / was going to happen*.

7 She promised *she'd help / helping / to help* me, but she never did!

4 ▶ 74 Listen and write the six sentences you hear.

5 Write a sentence before and after the sentences from Exercise 4 to create short dialogues.

6 Match the verbs (1–8) with the collocates (a–h).

1	campaign	a	a new player
2	break	b	bankrupt
3	forward	c	your collarbone
4	go	d	an email
5	hold	e	on some ice
6	sign	f	for civil rights
7	slip	g	a disease
8	cure	h	a summit

7 Decide if these words and phrases are connected to illness, accidents or news stories.

high blood pressure	bankrupt	badly burned
get bruised	slip over	have an affair
introduce a policy	crash	go on medication
under a lot of stress	sore throat	call a ceasefire

8 Complete the sentences. Use the word in brackets to form a word that fits in the space.

1 I read that the pilot lost _____ and that's what caused the crash. (conscious)

2 They need to _____ the whole system – and soon! (modern)

3 The two countries recently signed a new trade _____ . (agree)

4 Polio is a highly _____ disease. (infection)

5 The doctors said it was probably some kind of _____ reaction to something I'd eaten. (allergy)

6 They warned me that the pills could cause minor _____ to my eyes. (irritable)

7 Nicotine is highly _____ . (addiction)

8 He led the _____ struggle against England. (liberate)

9 Most diseases are _____ if they're treated early enough. (cure)

10 They've developed this amazing new _____ for addiction. (treat)

9 Complete the text with one word in each space. The first letters are given.

When I was in Texas, I had to go into hospital because I had a high ¹te_____ and quite a ²na_____ cough. I kept feeling a bit ³di_____ every time I stood up as well. The doctor that I saw told me there was a nasty ⁴vi_____ going around and gave me a check-up. Then he said that, judging by my symptoms, I probably just had flu and it should ⁵cl_____ up in a few days. He gave me an ⁶in_____ and then sent me home with some ⁷an_____ to take. I drank a lot of ⁸fl_____ and was soon feeling much better.

When I got the hospital bill, though, I nearly had a ⁹he_____ attack! I don't have any health insurance, but luckily I came into a bit of money when my grandfather died. He left me £2,000 in his ¹⁰wi_____ , so at least I was able to pay my bills.

SPEAKING

1 Work in groups. Discuss the questions.

- What things need doing when you organise the following?
  - a meeting
  - a wedding
  - a group excursion
  - a conference
  - a party
- Which is the most difficult thing to organise? Why?
- Have you ever been involved in organising any of these things? How easy was it?
- Did you have to make any changes or compromises?

WRITING

Fourteen 16-year-old schoolchildren are going on an exchange visit to Valencia, Spain. One of them has written to the organisation arranging the trip to ask to change the programme.

2 Read the email below. If you were Ms Roberts, would you agree to the change? Why? / Why not? What ways does Simon Holden use to try to persuade Ms Roberts?

3 Work in pairs. The email should have paragraphs to organise the different information and make it easier to read. Mark where you would start each new paragraph with //.

To   roberts14@ex-spain-ge.es
From   simonholden@exploremail.com

Dear Ms Roberts,

I am writing on **behalf** of the students who are going on the trip to Valencia in October. Firstly, can we say **thanks** for all your hard work organising the trip. On the **whole**, it looks great and we are all very much looking forward to it. However, we were **wondering** if we could possibly suggest one change. The Sunday after we arrive, there is a motorcycle Grand Prix in Cheste and ten of us would like to go. Currently, we are **scheduled** to go to the zoo that day and are free after lunch. Although we are sure the zoo is really nice, it seems a shame to miss such a big event while we are there, and Cheste is supposed to have a very special atmosphere. The four who are not interested in the motorcycling said they do not mind missing the zoo either. **Alternatively**, we could visit the zoo on Wednesday afternoon, which is currently free for shopping. We can take public transport to the Grand Prix as it is only 30km from Valencia. Obviously, we would pay for any extra cost, although we imagine you would have to come with us to supervise. We are sorry if this causes any **inconvenience**, but we are all very keen to go. We really hope that the change is possible and thank you again for all your work putting together the programme – we very much **appreciate** it. Yours sincerely,

Simon Holden

4 More formal writing has some rules such as those below. Find an example of each in the email.

1 Use surnames to address people.

2 Use full forms, not contractions (e.g. *did not* rather than *didn't*).

3 Avoid direct questions.

4 Use more formal words (e.g. *request* rather than *ask for*).

5 Use formal ways to sign off.

5 Look at the words in bold in the letter. Underline the whole chunk you could use for a similar letter.

6 Work in pairs. Cover the email and complete the extracts with one word in each space.

1 _____ _____ _____ _____ behalf _____ the students who are going on the trip to Valencia.

2 Firstly, _____ _____ _____ thanks _____ _____ _____ _____ _____ organising the trip.

3 _____ _____ whole, it looks great and we are all very much looking forward to it.

4 ... we _____ wondering _____ _____ _____ _____ suggest one change.

5 _____ , _____ _____ scheduled _____ go to the zoo ...

6 Alternatively, _____ _____ visit the zoo on Wednesday ...

7 We _____ _____ _____ _____ _____ _____ inconvenience, but we are all very keen to go.

8 Thank you again for all your work putting together the programme – _____ _____ _____ appreciate _____ .

KEYWORDS FOR WRITING

however, *although* and *but*

However, *although* and *but* can all have a similar meaning, but they use different grammar.

7 Look at these sentences from the email and complete the rules below.

a **Although** *we are sure the zoo is really nice, it seems a shame to miss such a big event.*

b *On the whole, it looks great and we are all really looking forward to it.* **However**, *we were wondering if we could possibly suggest one change.*

c *We are sorry if this causes any inconvenience,* **but** *we are all really keen to go.*

1 _____ and _____ connect two parts of the same sentence. _____ usually starts the sentence, but can come in the middle.

2 _____ always connects to an idea in a previous sentence. It usually starts the second sentence, but it can come in the middle or at the end of the second sentence.

8 Complete the sentences with one word in each space.

1 _____ it would be nice to visit the museum, we don't have enough time.

2 It's a very full programme. _____ , there is space for one more visit on Monday afternoon.

3 We would really like to go to the exhibition, _____ we were wondering if we could go on Tuesday instead of Sunday.

4 Thanks again for your help. _____ we realise these last minute changes are inconvenient, we are sure they will improve the programme.

5 On the whole, everything seems to be very clear. I do have couple of queries, _____ .

9 Rewrite each pair of sentences as one sentence using the words in brackets and the correct punctuation.

1 Giving all the participants a souvenir is a nice idea. It might be a bit too expensive. (but)

_____

2 I personally like rock music. Some of those attending might prefer something different. (although)

_____

3 The menu for the dinner looks great. I think we should have a better option for vegetarians. (however)

_____

VOCABULARY *Programme*

10 Complete the collocations with *programme* by using the correct form of these words.

exciting	include	put together
full	last-minute	swap

1 Thank you for all your hard work _____ the programme.

2 We were wondering if we could make two _____ changes to the programme.

3 Alternatively, we could _____ some things round in the programme.

4 Currently, it is a very _____ programme. Could we perhaps drop something from the programme and make room for some free time?

5 It looks like a very _____ programme of events and we are very much looking forward to it.

6 We regret to inform you we will be unable to _____ your talk in the programme.

PRACTICE

11 Work in pairs. Plan a week's programme for a group of exchange students visiting where you live or a programme of lectures and activities for a company team-building day.

12 Swap your programme from Exercise 11 with another pair. With your partner, discuss what you would change in the programme, why you would change it and how.

13 Write a formal email to the organisers to request your changes. Use as much of the language from this lesson as you can.

SPEAKING

1 **Work in pairs. Discuss the questions.**

- Look at the photos. What kind of age group do you think the activities / places are good for?
- What other activities / places are good for the following ages?
3–6	12–15
7–11	16–18
- What facilities are there for young people where you live? Do you think there are enough? Why? / Why not?

WRITING

2 **Read the report on the facilities for young people in a Spanish village called Rocafort. Then work in pairs and discuss the questions.**

- Do you think the area is better or worse for young people than where you live? Why?
- Can you think of any other services or facilities that could be provided for the young people of Rocafort?

CURRENT YOUTH PROVISION IN ROCAFORT

Introduction

At present, there are only a limited number of things for young people to do in Rocafort. As a result, the main free-time activity is simply hanging out in the street.

Sports

There is a small outdoor sports centre, which has a football pitch, a basketball court and two tennis courts. In addition, there is a swimming pool, although this is only open from July till the first week in August. Nearby, there is a small park with a climbing frame and swings.

Other activities

The village has a social centre that runs classes in dance and yoga two days a week. For younger children, there are painting classes. This centre also has a small cinema screen and auditorium. However, this is rarely used.

Recommendations

As far as classes are concerned, the council could provide a wider range for all age groups. For example, they could do drama or run music groups. More could be done with the cinema: why not show regular films on Friday evenings or Saturday mornings?

In terms of the sports facilities, the council could provide more organised teams and subsidise coaching sessions. Finally, the council should consider covering the swimming pool so it could be used in winter.

6 Work in pairs. Discuss the questions.

- Where do kids hang out in your town / area? Is it a problem?
- Does the government subsidise anything in your area?
- Are there any places / facilities you know which are underused? How could more be done with them?
- Is there anything your local council should consider doing?

KEY WORDS FOR WRITING

Referring to things

We often refer to particular things in a report using *as far as X is / are concerned* or *in terms of X*.

As far as classes are concerned, the council could provide a wider range for all age groups.

In terms of the sports facilities, the council could provide more organised teams.

7 Match the two parts of the sentences.

1 As far as public transport in the area is concerned,
2 In terms of the canteen,
3 As far as the hotel facilities are concerned,
4 In terms of security,
5 As far as the French classes are concerned,
6 In terms of the park,

a the number of students should be reduced.
b the owners should consider building a swimming pool.
c more could be done to stop robberies.
d most people are satisfied with the quality of food.
e there's a good range of play equipment for younger kids.
f many complain that the trains do not run late enough.

8 Think of the area where you live. Complete the sentences with your own ideas, explaining how people feel or how things could be different.

1 As far as public transport is concerned, …
2 As far as schools are concerned, …
3 In terms of sports facilities, …
4 In terms of things for young people, …

9 Work in pairs. Discuss your sentences from Exercise 8. Do you agree with your partner's ideas?

PRACTICE

10 Write a short report on one of the following.

- Facilities for young people the place where you live
- Public transport where you live
- Your school / university / workplace

Write about the current situation and make some recommendations about how things could be improved. Use the passive where appropriate and add suitable subheadings at the start of each new section.

3 Look at the report again. Underline all the examples of the passive that you can find. Then work in pairs and discuss why the passive is used in writing reports.

4 Find four ways of giving advice / making recommendations in the report.

VOCABULARY Describing facilities

5 Complete the sentences using words from the report.

1 There are only a limited _____ of classes you can go to.
2 The problem is that there's nowhere safe for kids to _____ out with their friends.
3 There are several squash _____ and table tennis tables.
4 The school _____ a drama club in the evenings. Anyone can go.
5 There is a sauna at the sports centre, but for some reason it is _____ used.
6 The cinema could put on a _____ range of films.
7 More could be _____ with the existing facilities – why not open them in the evenings?
8 The government should _____ swimming pools so everyone can afford to use them.
9 The council should _____ providing free sports equipment.

7 WRITING Opinion-led essays

SPEAKING

1 You are going to read a short essay about cars. First, work in pairs and discuss the questions.

- What kind of car do you / the people in your family have?
- Do you have a favourite kind of car?
- What is the traffic like where you live?
- Do you use the car much? To go where?

WRITING

2 Look at the essay title below. Write three reasons why people might agree with the statement in the title and three reasons why people might disagree.

'Cars are no longer the best means of transport.' How far do you agree with this statement?

Cars are good because ...	Cars aren't good because ...
1.	1.
2.	2.
3.	3.

3 Work in pairs and compare your ideas. Then discuss how far you agree with each of the reasons you thought of.

4 Read the essay. Does the writer think the same as you?

5 Complete the essay with these words.

obviously	However	Otherwise	Secondly
Firstly	thirdly	In conclusion	Personally

6 The list below contains six pieces of advice for writing essays. Find examples in the essay of where the writer follows each piece of advice.

DOS AND DON'TS FOR OPINION-LED ESSAYS

1 Show you know why the question is being asked by giving examples of current trends or problems connected to it.

2 Make your own opinion clear in your introduction.

3 Allow space for points of view you disagree with and explain why you disagree with them.

4 Use paragraphs.

5 Avoid using *you*. Use impersonal forms like *people* or *one*.

6 Do not use contractions like *it'll* or *that'd*. Use full forms instead.

GRAMMAR

Describing trends

We usually begin introductions to opinion-led essays by describing trends or problems connected to the title. This helps to show the reader we understand why this question is important. To describe trends, we often use a 'double' comparative.

*Traffic is getting **worse and worse** every year.*

*Cycling is becoming **more and more popular**.*

***More and more people** are moving out of the city.*

***Fewer and fewer people** have driven to work as a result of the congestion charge.*

The number of cars on our roads has increased a lot over the last twenty years. Traffic is getting worse and worse every year and we are slowly running out of oil. As such, it is worth asking if cars are still the best way to travel. [1]_____ , I do not believe they are.

There are several reasons why cars remain so widely used. [2]_____ , they allow one to get directly from A to B. [3]_____ , people feel comfortable in their cars and [4]_____ , the car industry is a large employer and has influence with the government.

[5]_____ , in the long term we [6]_____ need to find alternatives to the car. [7]_____ , we will end up unable to move round our cities, as our streets become full of traffic. Road deaths will increase and there will be terrible environmental damage. It is time to limit car use and to encourage greater use of public transport and bicycles.

[8]_____ , while car users may want to continue using their vehicles, other options must be explored more fully.

7 Complete the introduction sentences below by making 'double' comparatives with these words. The first one is done for you.

bad	expensive	less	more
cheap	few	long	old

1 As property becomes *more and more expensive*, children are living at home _____ , with the average home-leaving age now well over 30.

2 Public transport has improved dramatically over the last few years. Despite this, _____ people are driving into the city centre to work every day.

3 Crime is getting _____ at the moment. The government recently increased the amount of money available to the police, but this has not made much difference.

4 We are constantly demanding _____ food. As financial pressures grow, animals are given _____ space to live in and the risk of diseases resulting from poor conditions is growing every year.

5 _____ people are having children these days. The average age to become a mother is getting _____ . As such, the birth rate is dropping quite dramatically.

8 Work in pairs. Discuss which trends in Exercise 7 are the same in your country – or how they are different.

9 Write similar introduction sentences to those in Exercise 7 for the two essay titles below.

'The Internet has destroyed both jobs and profits for far too many people.' Discuss.

'Fast food is having a terrible effect on the health of the nation. As such, it should be banned.' Do you agree?

KEY WORDS FOR WRITING

as such

To introduce results or conclusions, we often use *as such*. It means 'because what has just been said is true'. It usually begins a sentence and is followed by a comma.

Traffic is getting worse and worse every year and we are slowly running out of oil. **As such,** *it is worth asking if cars are still the best way to travel.*

10 Match sentences 1–5 with the results / conclusions a–e.

1 Many people nowadays are too busy to meet potential partners in the traditional way.

2 The war had become one disaster after another.

3 Over the last few years, the company has decided to do a lot more e-marketing.

4 More and more people are suffering from depression.

5 The school had the best results in the country last year.

a As such, sales have grown dramatically.

b As such, it is important to learn from its success.

c As such, Internet dating is growing in popularity.

d As such, the decision was made to bring the army home.

e As such, research into the factors affecting happiness has become more and more important.

11 Work in pairs. Think of one more possible sentence that could follow each sentence 1–5 in Exercise 10. Start each one with *As such*.

PRACTICE

12 Work in pairs. Choose either the title below or one of the titles in Exercise 9. Discuss possible reasons why people might agree or disagree with the main statement in the title you choose. Then discuss your own opinions.

'Some sports and entertainment stars earn far too much money.' How far do you agree with this statement?

13 Plan the content of each of your paragraphs. Use the model essay in this lesson to help you.

14 Write the essay. Use between 150 and 180 words. Use as much language from this lesson as you can.

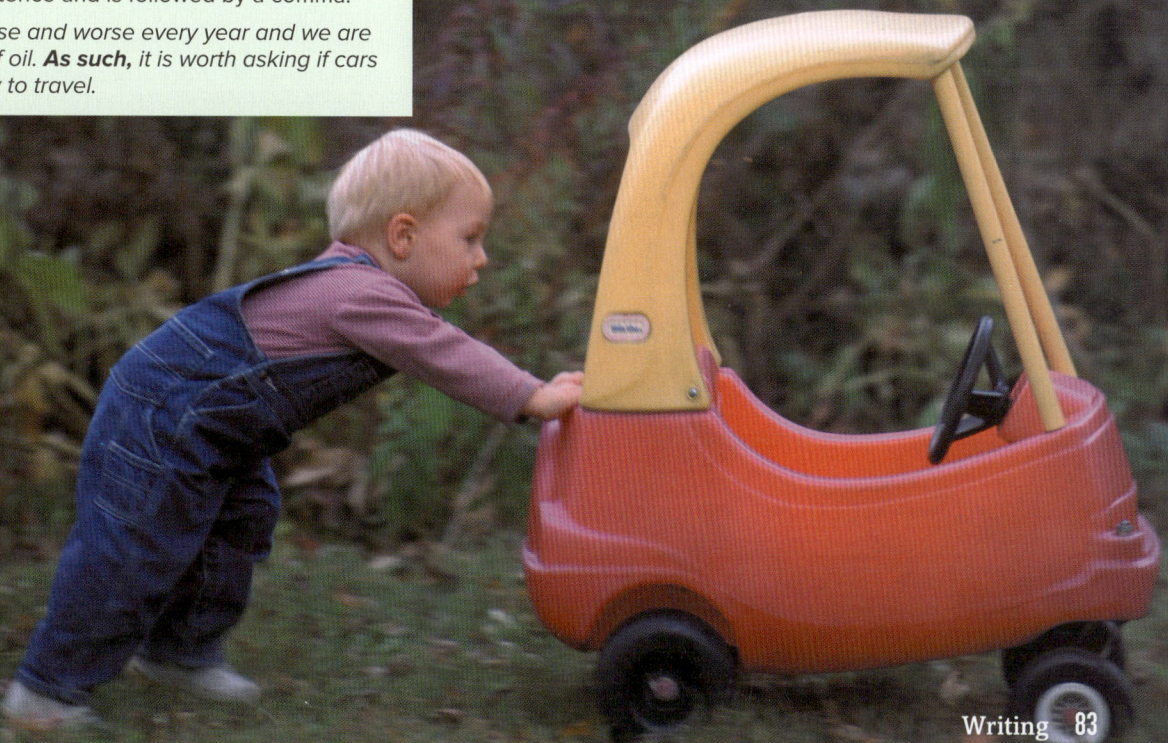

8 WRITING Reviews

SPEAKING

1 Work in groups. Discuss the questions.

- How often do you watch films?
- What kinds of films do you usually enjoy watching?
- Are there any kinds of films you usually avoid? Why?
- Do you prefer to watch films at the cinema or at home? Why?
- How do you decide what film you want to watch? Do you ever read reviews?
- Have you ever been given a recommendation which turned out to be a bad one?

VOCABULARY Describing films

2 Match the descriptions below to these words.

moving	gripping	entertaining
uplifting	hilarious	scary

1 I couldn't stop laughing. It's great.
2 It's so sad! I was in tears at the end of the film.
3 Some scenes make you jump out of your seat and it could give you nightmares!
4 It's really exciting. You just never know what's going to happen next.
5 Although she has a difficult life, the film leaves you feeling really happy and positive. It's a very inspiring story.
6 I enjoyed it. It's a fun film. It's got everything – a great cast of actors, lots of action, a good soundtrack.

3 Complete the sentences below with these words.

acted	chosen	directed
filmed	set	written

1 The film is _____ in Belfast in the early 1970s.
2 The main character is superbly _____ by Leonardo DiCaprio.
3 It has a very well-_____ script, full of jokes.
4 The mountains and countryside are beautifully _____ .
5 The film is brilliantly _____ by David Fincher.
6 The soundtrack contains several well-_____ songs, which really remind you of the time the film is set in.

4 Choose four adjectives from Exercises 2 and 3. Use them to tell a partner about films you know.

WRITING

5 Read this online article recommending three films. Then work in pairs and answer the questions.

1 Have you seen any of the films? Do you agree with the descriptions?
2 Would you like to see any of the films? Why? / Why not?
3 What tense is used to describe the plot in each review?
4 Are you told the whole plot? If not, why not?
5 Can you find eight adverb + adjective collocations in the three reviews?

FILM ONLINE

SEARCH

HOME   MOVIE NEWS   REVIEWS   BLOGS

Three all-time favourites

LIFE IS BEAUTIFUL (LA VITA È BELLA)
★ ★ ★ ★ ★

This is a strangely uplifting film directed by and starring Roberto Benigni. It tells the story of an Italian man and his son who are sent to a concentration camp during the Second World War. While they are there, the father distracts the boy from all the bad things that are happening by turning their life into a game. The film has everything: it's funny, heartbreaking, superbly written and beautifully filmed.

SEVEN PSYCHOPATHS
★ ★ ★ ★ ★

When this thoroughly entertaining film begins, we see the Hollywood sign in the hills of Los Angeles, and it's very much about the whole process of creating movies. It features a well-chosen cast and stars Colin Farrell, who is a writer working on a film called … *Seven Psychopaths*! As part of his research, Farrell meets all kinds of strange people and the line between life and art becomes increasingly unclear. The film manages to be hilarious, complex and clever. I can't recommend it enough.

12 YEARS A SLAVE
★ ★ ★ ★ ★

The historical drama *12 Years a Slave* is a remarkable film about the experiences of Solomon Northrup, a free black man who was kidnapped while he was living in New York and then sold into slavery. The film is based on a true story and is both gripping and extremely moving. Directed by British filmmaker Steve McQueen, it's not an easy watch as it's very violent in places. However, it's a powerful story that is incredibly well acted.

KEY WORDS FOR WRITING

while, when and *during*

While, *when* and *during* show how two or more actions relate to each other in time. *While* and *during* introduce a continuing action or a period of time in which another action happens. *While* is followed by a clause (often using the past continuous). *During* is followed by a noun.

*... a free black man who was kidnapped **while he was living in New York**.*

*It tells the story of an Italian man and his son who are sent to a concentration camp **during the Second World War**.*

When introduces a finished action. It is usually followed by a clause using the present or past simple.

***When** this thoroughly entertaining film begins, we see the Hollywood sign in the hills of Los Angeles ...*

Note that you can also use *when* instead of *while* for continuous actions, but *while* is more common.

6 **Decide if both options are possible in each sentence. If not, choose the correct option.**

1 The film takes place *during* / *when* the Gulf War in 1990.
2 They fall in love *when* / *while* she is planning his wedding!
3 *While* / *During* she's not looking, he puts a drug in her drink.
4 *While* / *During* the night, the toys come alive.
5 Things start to go wrong *when* / *while* the main character decides to change his name.
6 *While* / *During* the parents are away, he has to defend the house against robbers.

GRAMMAR
Adding information after nouns

7 **Read the Grammar box. Then match each sentence a–f to one of the three ways (1–3) we add information after nouns.**

We often add information after nouns in three different ways:

1 by using *-ed* / *-ing* participles

   *This is a strangely uplifting **film directed by** and **starring** Roberto Benigni.*

2 by adding a prepositional phrase

   The historical drama 12 Years A Slave *is a **remarkable film about the experiences of Solomon Northrup**.*

3 by using relative clauses

   *It features a well-chosen cast and stars **Colin Farrell, who is a writer** ...*

a This is a moving love story about *a disabled woman*.
b This is a comedy action film starring *Akshay Kumar*.
c The film is directed by Lasse Hallstrom, who also directed *The Cider House Rules*.
d The film is set in a small town during *the mayoral election*.
e The main character is a *brilliant but lonely doctor* superbly played by *Jennifer Jenkins*.
f The documentary follows the lives of *four couples* who have recently *emigrated to Australia*.

8 **Work in pairs. Replace the words in italics in the sentences in Exercise 8 with ideas of your own. Think of two possible alternatives for each sentence.**

PRACTICE

9 **A film magazine has a competition inviting readers to send in a review of three films. Each week they publish one winner. Write your entry for one of the choices below. Use between 180 and 225 words.**

   • Three best films of last year
   • Three films for a Sunday afternoon with the family
   • Three classics
   • Three films for three different moods

GRAMMAR REFERENCE

9 HOUSES

PRESENT PERFECT SIMPLE AND PRESENT PERFECT CONTINUOUS

The present perfect simple (*have / has* + (*not*) + past participle) is often used to talk about trends continuing from the past to now. We often use an adverb to say how quickly the change happened, or by how much. We use a time phrase to show the period of time.

Unemployment has House prices have	risen increased gone up gone down dropped fallen	dramatically sharply a lot steadily gradually slightly a bit by 15%	over the past few months. over the last few years. over the past ten years. in recent months. in recent years. since last year. since the last election.

Continuous or simple?

We also use the continuous form (*have / has* + (*not*) + *been* + *-ing*) to talk about trends continuing from the past to now. The continuous form can be used to emphasise the duration of an activity or the fact that it is regularly repeated.

Unemployment **has been rising** *over the last year.*

House prices **have been falling steadily.**

The situation **has been gradually improving** *over recent months.*

We don't use the continuous form when showing quick changes or to say exactly how much.

The price of oil ~~has been increasing~~ **has increased** *dramatically.*

Inflation ~~has been falling~~ **has fallen** *by 3% this year.*

We also use the simple form for finished changes / events that took place at some point before now.

They **have built** *6,000 new houses in our city in the last two years.* (= already built)

I've seen *one or two places on sale with a discount.* (= in the past, before now)

Exercise 1

Decide if both forms are possible in each sentence. If not, choose the correct option.

1 Inflation *has been gradually falling / has gradually fallen* over the last two years.
2 The population *has grown / has been growing* dramatically in recent years.
3 The government *has introduced / has been introducing* laws in the last year to prevent foreigners buying property and leaving it empty.
4 More and more people *have been leaving / have left* the country because of the economic problems.
5 Unemployment *has increased / has been increasing* by 6% since the crash.
6 Things *have improved / have been improving* slowly over the last few years.

7 We *have moved / have been moving* house three times in the last five years.
8 I've been under a bit of stress, because *I've moved / I've been moving* house recently.

Exercise 2

Complete the sentences with one word in each space. Sometimes more than one answer is possible.

1 The crime rate has _____ falling steadily over the last twenty years.
2 Unemployment has risen sharply _____ the start of the economic crisis.
3 The birth rate has fallen _____ from 2.4 to 2.1 over the last decade.
4 In the last decade, the population has grown _____ 25% to reach 100 million people.
5 Oil prices have _____ dramatically in _____ months. It was $125 a barrel at the beginning of the year and now it's $80.
6 House prices _____ more or less stayed the same _____ the _____ two years.

COMPARING NOW AND THE PAST

Comparisons with nouns

We can use *more* with any kind of noun.

We use *fewer* or *not as many* with plural countable nouns.

We use *less* or *not as much* with uncountable nouns.

We often make comparatives between now and the past using the following patterns.

There are	(many) more (far) fewer	cars on the road bars in the area	than	before. in the past.
There aren't	(nearly) as many	schools here working-class people	as	there were. there used to be.
There is	(much) more (far) less	pollution car crime	than	there was when I was a kid.
There isn't	as much	investment news on TV	as	there was 20 years ago.

Note that we more commonly start with the present situation, but we can also start with the past.

There **were** *fewer problems in the past than there* **are** *now.*

Twenty years ago, parents **spent** *more time with their children (than they* **do** *now).*

Comparisons with adjectives

We also compare the past and present using comparative adjectives.

The area is **more popular** *with young people than* **it used to be.**

That part of town used to be **much rougher** *than* **it is** *now.*

I'm **not as fit as** *I was when* **I was** *at university.*

Exercise 1

There is one word missing in each sentence. Add the word in the correct place.

1 It's far multicultural than it was ten years ago.
2 It wasn't nice as the last time we went there.
3 There aren't as people living here as when I was a kid.

4 There's less unemployment there used to be.
5 There are more restaurants than were before.
6 The area isn't as working class as used to be.
7 There isn't as pollution round here since the government tightened the laws.
8 There didn't use to be as many shops here as there now.

Using auxiliary verbs in comparisons

Notice that the second auxiliary verb in comparisons might be different to the first.

*The area **has** more cultural events than it **did** before.*

*It**'s** not as interesting as it **was** twenty years ago.*

Exercise 2

Complete the sentences below with these verbs.

used to be	can	do	did	were	is

1 It's not as difficult to get round the city as it _____ .
2 There are so many more cars on the street than there _____ a few years ago.
3 I used to work a lot harder than I _____ now.
4 We spend less money at the supermarket than we _____ in the past.
5 Before they changed the laws, we could work more hours per week than we _____ now.
6 It never used to be as multicultural as it _____ now.

10 GOING OUT

QUANTIFIERS

We use quantifiers when we want to give information about the number or amount of something.

not any	no	*There are **no** cinemas nearby.* *There are**n't any** cinemas nearby.*
hardly any almost no	(very) few (very) little	***Few** / **Hardly any** locals can afford to go to the top restaurants.* *I heard it can be dangerous, but we saw **almost no** / **very little** trouble.*
some	a few a little not much not many	*A lot of us went home, but **some** / **a few** people went on to a club.* *I don**'t** drink **much**, but I may have **some** / **a little** wine at dinner.* *There were**n't many** people there.* ***Some**, but I expected more.* *There is**n't much** nightlife here.* *There are **a few** places, but there could be more.*
a lot of	(so) many (so) much	***A lot of** / **many** people are living in poverty.* *Apparently, things are expensive because there's **a lot of** / **so much** corruption.*
almost all almost every	most	***Almost all** / **Most** clubs charge you to get in. Hardly any have free entry.* ***Almost every** place we went to had a TV with a fashion channel on.*
all / every		*The DJ plays **all** kinds of music.* ***Every** time I go out someone hassles me!*

few and many, little and much

(A) few and *many* go with plural countable nouns, e.g. *people, cinemas, locals*, etc.

(A) little and *much* go with uncountable nouns, e.g. *money, corruption, poverty*, etc.

We often use these quantifiers with *so*. They often link a cause and result.

*We have **so much** daylight in the summer that it's difficult to sleep sometimes.*

*There was no real atmosphere in the place because there were **so few** people.*

a few and few, a little and little

A few and *a little* generally have a more positive meaning than *few* and *little*.

*I had **a little break** and took **a few days** off work.*

*I have **little time** to myself, so I know **few people** here.*

no and not

We cannot use *not* directly before a noun – we have to use *no* or *not any*.

*I ~~haven't~~ **have no** / **don't have any** idea where it is.*

*There ~~aren't~~ **are no** / **aren't any** clubs round here.*

all and every

We can use *all* with singular and plural nouns. We usually use a determiner such as *the, my, your* or *these* with plural nouns. We use *every* only with singular nouns.

*The party lasted **all** day and all night. (= the whole day / night)*

*We saw **all the sites** while we were there.*

*We visited **every museum** and gallery in the city!*

DID YOU KNOW?

In spoken language, we usually use *a lot* in positive sentences. We generally use *much* and *many* in negative sentences or with *so* (see above). However, in formal or academic writing, *much* and *many* are often used in positive sentences.

Exercise 1

Complete the text with one word in each space.

I live in a fairly small place in Chile, so there's [1]_____ entertainment at night. There are a [2]_____ bars, but only one is open late and they don't play [3]_____ music that I like. So [4]_____ weekends, I travel to Santiago where there are a [5]_____ of clubs playing [6]_____ kinds of music, such as Salsa, Reggaeton and Pop. Personally, I'm a big fan of electronic dance music and there's a growing scene in Santiago. It's mainly Chilean DJs playing in the clubs, but we get [7]_____ international DJs coming over and there's also a big festival – Sensation – [8]_____ year. I'd like to move to Santiago soon, because I spend so [9]_____ time there, but there are [10]_____ jobs available at the moment so I'll have to see.

DID YOU KNOW?

When we use nouns with *the* or pronouns after some quantifiers, we add *of* after the quantifier.

*some **of** us, (a) few **of** them,*

*most **of** the time, many **of** the best restaurants*

Exercise 2

Complete the second sentence so that it has a similar meaning to the first sentence using the word given. Do not change the word given. You must use between three and four words, including the word given.

1 I went to the cinema with several friends last night.
  US
  A _____ to the cinema last night.
2 We could hardly move because the place was packed.
  PEOPLE
  There _____ there, we could hardly move.

3 There won't be anything to eat at the party.
 FOOD
 There'll _____ at the party.
4 Crime is almost non-existent, so you can walk safely at night.
 VERY
 You can walk safely at night as there _____ crime.
5 A lot of restaurants in town have discounts for students.
 MANY
 If you're a student, you can get a discount at _____ town's restaurants.

THE FUTURE IN THE PAST

Plans and intentions

We often use the structure *was / were going to* + infinitive (without *to*) to talk about things that were planned or intended, but then didn't happen. To explain why, we often add a clause starting with *but*.

I *was going to go* swimming after work yesterday, *but* in the end I was too tired.

Some friends *were going to come* for dinner, *but* they rang to say they couldn't make it.

I *was* just *going to go* out for a walk when it started pouring with rain.

Promises and predictions

We often use *would(n't)* + infinitive (without *to*) to talk about promises and predictions in the past – especially ones that didn't then happen or come true. We also usually use another verb in the past simple in the same sentence.

He *promised* he *wouldn't be* late. (but he was late / but he is late now)
(His actual words were probably 'I won't be late.')

I *said* I'd *go* with her. (but you didn't!)
(Your actual words were probably 'I'll go with you.')

The play *was* better than I *thought* it *would be*.
(My actual thought was 'I don't think it'll be very good.')

I *didn't think* it'd *be* anything special. (but it was)
(My actual thought was 'I don't think it will be anything special.' / 'It won't be anything special.')

Exercise 1

Complete the exchanges with one word in each space.

1 A: So did you go and see that film last night?
 B: No, I was going [1]_____ , but I had an essay to hand in and it took longer than I thought it [2]_____ , so by the time I'd finished, it [3]_____ too late.
2 A: What did you do at the weekend?
 B: Nothing much. We [1]_____ going to go to the beach, but the weather was so awful, we just stayed at home.
 A: I know. It was terrible, wasn't it? It was so annoying, because the forecast said it [2]_____ be sunny!
3 A: So how was your holiday? Did you go away anywhere?
 B: Bad question, I'm afraid! You see, me and my brother [1]_____ going to go to visit our uncle in Spain. He'd promised he [2]_____ pay for the flights, but in the end he said he couldn't afford it, so we just had to [3]_____ at home instead.

Exercise 2

Complete the second sentence so that it has a similar meaning to the first sentence using the word given. You must use between three and five words, including the word given.

1 A friend rang and said he had tickets for the Slayer concert, which is why I didn't stay in.
 OUT
 I was _____ , but a friend gave me a ticket for the Slayer concert.

2 I expected him to be rubbish, but he was actually quite good.
 THOUGHT
 His performance was much better _____ be.
3 It's so sunny! The forecast was for rain.
 IT
 They said _____ , but it's turned out really nice.
4 My dad promised to help me later.
 SAID
 He _____ me later.
5 The government has broken their promise not to raise taxes.
 INCREASE
 At the election, the government said _____ , but they have.
6 I feel a bit guilty about not going to the party because I promised to be there.
 DEFINITELY
 I told her _____ at the party, so I feel guilty that I haven't gone.

11 THE NATURAL WORLD

PAST ABILITY / OBLIGATION

could

With sense verbs (*see, hear, feel, smell, taste*), we usually use *could(n't)* + infinitive (without *to*) rather than *managed to*.
We ~~managed to~~ *could hear* these little cries coming from somewhere, but we *couldn't see* her anywhere.
When I walked in, I ~~managed to~~ *could* immediately *smell* gas.

We also use *could* to talk about general abilities in the past.
I *could ride* a horse by the time I was five.
He *could make* these crazy noises like a dog! It was really funny.

couldn't / could hardly

We use *couldn't* or *could hardly* to show it wasn't possible to do something in a specific situation.
We *couldn't see* her anywhere. (= It wasn't possible for us to see her.)
I chased it for ages, but I just *couldn't catch* it. (= It wasn't possible.)
I was so nervous I *could hardly say* a word.

Note that we can also use *didn't manage to* or *hardly managed to* in these situations. However, these structures are less commonly used than *could / could hardly*.

managed to

We use *managed to* + infinitive (without *to*) – not *could* – to show an ability to do something difficult in a specific situation.
When it came down, I ~~could~~ *managed to catch* it and put it into a box.
The fire service took ages trying to get the cat out of the tree, but they ~~could~~ *managed to do* it in the end.
I screamed and screamed and eventually I ~~could~~ *managed to attract* someone's attention.

Note how *managed to* often goes with words and phrases such as *finally*, *in the end* and *eventually*.

DID YOU KNOW?

We often use *managed to* when talking about stupid mistakes.
I *managed to lose* my passport somehow.
We *managed to get ripped off* everywhere we went.

had to

We use *had to* + infinitive (without *to*) – not *must* – to show we felt there was no other choice.

We **had to call** the fire services.

I **had to put** some fruit and seeds on the ground to tempt it down.

I **couldn't see** the monkeys so I **had to sit** on my boyfriend's shoulders.

Exercise 1

Complete the sentences with *could, couldn't, managed to* **or** *had to*.

1 I was cycling along and this dog suddenly chased after me, but I just _____ cycle fast enough to escape.
2 We went on a whale watching trip, but we _____ see anything because the weather was terrible.
3 It was a bit scary camping at night, because you _____ actually hear wolves howling in the distance!
4 It got so dark we _____ hardly see anything. I'm amazed we _____ get down the mountain without falling.
5 My dog was making such a dreadful noise I _____ lock him inside a room so the neighbours _____ hear.
6 There were cockroaches in the house and I _____ get rid of them, so in the end we _____ call a specialist to deal with the problem.
7 There were so many people on the train, you _____ really move, but I actually _____ get a seat in the end. I was really lucky.
8 The car broke down in the middle of nowhere and I _____ get it to start, then we _____ wait for ages for the breakdown service to come.

PASSIVES

Passives allow us to emphasise the person or thing an action is done to. We make passive sentences with a form of the verb *be* + past participle. Passives can be used in different tenses.

Present simple

*Most of the coal **is exported**.*

*Over 3,000 people **are employed** in the mine.*

Present continuous

*More gas than ever **is being exported** from the country.*

*Many people believe that prices **are being controlled** by the major suppliers.*

Past simple

*A lot of money **was stolen** by corrupt politicians.*

*During the civil war thousands of people **were killed**.*

Past continuous

*About 80% of the oil **was being sold**, the rest **was being kept**.*

*The government was worried that diamonds **were being exported** illegally.*

Present perfect simple

*The profits from oil **have been invested** in health care.*

*Oil **has been discovered** in the north of the country.*

DID YOU KNOW?

We don't usually make passives in the present perfect continuous.

Modal verbs

To make passives after a modal verb, use *be* + past participle.

*The resources there **can** now **be extracted** more easily.*

*Most natural resources **will be used up** in the next 50 years.*

*More **should be done** to help developing countries.*

by

You can introduce who or what did the action using the word *by* after the verb.

*The phrase 'the resource curse' was first used **by** the writer Richard Auty.*

However, we often don't mention who or what did an action because:

1 it is not clear or not known.
   *Oil **has been discovered** in the north.* (= We don't know who by.)
2 it is obvious.
   *Most of the coal **is exported**.* (by the companies who mine it)
   *Taxes **are not being spent** wisely.* (by the government)

Exercise 1

Choose the correct option.

I recently [1]*attended / was attended* a conference on how profits from the sale of natural resources can best [2]*use / be used* for human development. It's an important question because oil and gas have recently [3]*discovered / been discovered* in many African countries, including Ghana, Uganda and Kenya. In many sub-Saharan countries, natural resources have [4]*managed / been managed* very badly for too many years, and people in many resource-rich countries often still [5]*receive / are received* worse educations and health care than people in countries without resources.

Interestingly, I learned that in many countries with lots of natural resources, people [6]*aren't taxed / don't tax* very much. As a result, they [7]*aren't expected / don't expect* much from their governments in return. They pay less and so they have less reason to worry about how their money [8]*spends / is spent*. This leaves politicians free to keep the money that has [9]*earned / been earned* by selling the natural resources. Sadly, if people do complain, the government often uses oil or gas money to [10]*pay / be paid* the army to stop any protests.

Exercise 2

Complete the second sentence so that it has a similar meaning to the first sentence using the word given. Do not change the word given. You must use between three and four words, including the word given.

1 They discovered oil there back in the 1970s.
   WAS
   _____ back in the 1970s.
2 The government subsidises petrol prices, which is why they are so low.
   BY
   Petrol is so cheap there because _____ the government.
3 There's a lot of pollution in the rivers because of the mining.
   BADLY
   The rivers have _____ because of the mining.
4 The government could do more to stop corruption if it wanted to.
   DONE
   More _____ stop corruption if the government wanted to.

5 They are building a new motorway which will destroy the area.
BUILT
The area will be destroyed by this new motorway _____ .
6 They should do more to prevent people cutting down trees illegally.
BEING
More should be done to prevent _____ illegally.

12 PEOPLE I KNOW

USED TO, WOULD AND PAST SIMPLE

Habits and regular events

We can use all three forms: *used to* + infinitive (without *to*), *would* + infinitive (without *to*) and the past simple to talk about habits or regular events in the past. Often these habits / events no longer happen now.

Would is more common than *used to*. We often start with *used to* and then give extra details using *would*.

He **smoked** a pipe. I **used to love** the smell of the fresh tobacco. I'**d** sometimes even **open** the tin when he **wasn't** there to smell it.

We **used to live** next door to my cousins so we'**d spend** a lot of time together. We'**d play** together most days in the street in front of our block of flats.

Negatives

All of the following are commonly used by native speakers, though some people say the last form is incorrect. In exams, it's best to avoid it, but don't be surprised if you hear or see it used.

My grandparents **never used to visit** us. We'd always go to their house.

My grandparents **didn't use to visit** us. We'd always go to their house.

My grandparents **didn't used to visit** us. We'd always go to their house.

Past state

We talk about past states with the past simple or *used to* – not *would*.

I **loved** / **used to love** the smell of fresh tobacco.

He **had** / **used to have** long white hair.

I **belonged** / **used to belong** to a gym, but I never went, so I stopped paying in the end.

Single events

We only use the past simple for single events.

When he ~~used to die~~ **died**, Gran ~~would move~~ **moved** to a town by the seaside.

They ~~used to get~~ **got** married and ~~would have~~ **had** their first child a year later.

Exercise 1

Decide if both forms are possible in each sentence. If not, choose the correct option.

A: Arnedo's a lovely place, isn't it? How do you know it?
B: Well, my parents [1]*used to have / would have* a little house near there. We [2]*would go / went* there every summer for a month.
A: Really? Whereabouts?
B: The house [3]*was / would be* just outside the town.
A: Lovely. Did you [4]*use to go / go* walking round there?
B: Not really. In fact, we [5]*would never / never used to* do much while we were there. We [6]*would go / went* swimming in the river, we [7]*went / used to go* for bike rides, but to be honest, none of us were into walking.

A: Oh, OK. So how come your parents [8]*used to sell / sold* the house?
B: Well, as we [9]*would get / got* older, we used to complain so much about going they [10]*would decide / decided* to sell it.

EXPRESSING REGRET USING *WISH*

We use the past perfect simple (*had* + past participle) after *wish* to express regret about things in the past. To express regret about things that didn't happen, but that we wanted to happen, we use *wish* + *had* + past participle.

I **wish** I'**d been** a bit stricter with my children. (= I was quite indulgent with them and they became spoilt.)

To express regret about things that did happen, but that we didn't want to happen, use *wish* + *hadn't* + past participle.

I **wish** I **hadn't eaten** so much. (= I ate a lot and now I feel sick.)

Exercise 1

Choose the correct option.

1 I often wish I *had / hadn't* travelled more when I had the chance, but it's impossible with the children.
2 I wish I *had / hadn't* gone. It was such a waste of time.
3 All the flights are really expensive. I wish I *had / hadn't* left it till the last minute to book them.
4 I wish I *had / hadn't* brought up my children in the country. It's healthier and they would've had more freedom.
5 I wish I *had / hadn't* ignored him. He was right.
6 Thanks. You've been really helpful. I wish I *had / hadn't* spoken to you earlier.
7 I really shouted at her and I wish I *had / hadn't* now.
8 I never really pushed my children very hard, but I sometimes wish I *had / hadn't*. They would've thanked me for it.

DID YOU KNOW?

There are other common ways of expressing regret.

I really **regret** not ask**ing** for her phone number. (= I wish I'd asked her for her phone number.)

It's a shame I didn't think of that. (= I wish I'd thought of that.)

Exercise 2

Complete the second sentence so that it has a similar meaning to the first sentence.

1 I really regret starting smoking.
I really wish _____ .
2 I really regret not asking her.
I wish _____ .
3 It's a shame you didn't tell me.
I wish _____ .
4 I regret being so hard on my children.
I wish _____ .
5 It's a shame I lost touch with them.
I really wish _____ .
6 It's a shame I didn't move when I had the chance.
I wish _____ .

13 JOURNEYS

THIRD CONDITIONALS

We use third conditionals to talk about imagined past situations. To form third conditionals, use the past perfect in the *if*-clause. The other clause shows the possible results or consequences of the *if*-clause. We use *would* + *have* + past participle if the consequence seems definite. We use *could* (or *might*) + *have* + past participle if the consequence seems only possible.

Either clause can come first. When the *if*-clause comes first, add a comma after it.

Compare these examples with the real situations given in brackets.

*If he **hadn't been** so determined, Hussain **could** easily **have given up** and returned home.*

(= He was really determined and so he didn't give up and go home. He continued with his journey.)

*If I**'d stayed** in Afghanistan, none of this **would've happened**.*

(= He didn't stay in Afghanistan. He moved to Australia, where he set up his own business.)

Exercise 1

Complete the sentences with the correct form of the verbs.

1 I _____ you last night if I _____ your number. (call, had)

2 I _____ if I _____ she was going to be here. (not / come, know)

3 If you _____ your bag in such a stupid place, I _____ over it. (not / leave, not / trip)

4 We _____ lost if the battery on my phone _____ . (not / get, not / die)

5 There's no way I _____ my own business if I _____ in my own country. It just _____ possible. (set up, stay, not / be)

6 If there _____ so much traffic on the way to the airport, I _____ that plane which crashed, and I wouldn't be here today! (not / be, catch)

DID YOU KNOW?

Although we usually use the past perfect simple in *if*-clauses, we can also use the past perfect continuous (*had been* + *-ing*) to talk about actions that happened over an extended period of time.

*If he**'d been driving** a bit slower, he **wouldn't have crashed**.*

(= He was driving really fast and that's why he crashed.)

*We **might never have met** if I **hadn't been working** that day.*

(= I was working and on that day, we met.)

Exercise 2

Decide which six sentences are incorrect then correct them.

1 If you'd asked me earlier, I could come yesterday, but I didn't have time to rearrange my meeting.

2 If we would set off at ten instead of eight, we would've missed the rush hour.

3 It would've been worse if she hadn't been wearing a seatbelt.

4 I don't know what I would've did if I hadn't come here.

5 If it hadn't been for that long journey, we might never have got to know each other.

6 If there'd been a traffic jam, I might've got there on time.

7 We wouldn't have got lost if we'd given better directions.

8 My career would have been ended if I hadn't had that operation.

SHOULD HAVE

We use *should've / shouldn't have* + past participle to talk about things that went wrong in the past.

Should've explains good things that people failed to do or were unable to do. *Shouldn't have* explains things people did which were bad. There is often a present reason for stating these regrets.

*My mobile's dead. I **should've recharged** it before I left.*

*I overslept. I **should've set** my alarm clock.*

*I **shouldn't have eaten** so much earlier. I feel dreadful.*

You can also use *never* to make a negative.

*I **should never have started** smoking!*

DID YOU KNOW?

We prefer to use *so* instead of *very* after *shouldn't have*.

*He shouldn't have been driving **so** fast.*

*I shouldn't have eaten **so** much.*

Exercise 1

Complete the sentences using *should've / shouldn't have* and the past participle of the verbs.

1 It's crazy! They _____ so many people onto the ferry. (let)

2 Look at the traffic! I knew we _____ the train. (take)

3 We _____ somewhere else. It was a rip-off. (go)

4 It's my own fault. I _____ to overtake on such a tight corner. (try)

5 You _____ me you were having difficulties. I could've helped you. (told)

6 It's my fault. I _____ so stupid. (be)

Continuous and passive

We also use *should've* and *shouldn't have* with continuous or passive forms of the verb.

*You **should've been working**, not surfing the Web.* (You weren't working when he saw you.)

*They **shouldn't have been arrested** for demonstrating against the government.*

Exercise 2

Complete the second sentence so that it has a similar meaning to the first sentence.

1 We didn't set off early enough.
It was silly. We _____ earlier.

2 I wish I hadn't left it till the last minute.
I should _____ till the last minute.

3 It's a shame you didn't come to the party. It was great.
You _____ party. You would've enjoyed it

4 Nobody told us about the change until it was too late.
We really _____ about the change sooner.

5 I'm not surprised you fell over if you were looking behind you.
It's your own fault you fell. You _____ where you were going!

6 If you hadn't been in such a rush, you wouldn't have crashed the car.
It's your fault you crashed. You _____ fast.

14 TECHNOLOGY

ARTICLES

Indefinite articles: *a / an*

We use *a* (or *an* if the following word starts with a vowel):

1 to say what someone is.

*I'm **a computer engineer.***

*I'm **a programmer**.*

*It's strange to think I'm now **a grandmother**.*

*You're **an idiot**!*

2 before nouns when they are one of several, when it's not important which one we mean, or when we mention something for the first time.

*The feeling of landing **a passenger jet** safely is incredibly exciting.* (= It doesn't matter which passenger jet. All jets are exciting to land.)

*Internet speeds and connectivity are still **a real issue** in many areas here.* (= There are lots of other issues too. This is one among many.)

*One part of **a game** was released later than promised.* (= This is the first time this game has been mentioned – and it doesn't matter which game.)

Note that we do not use indefinite articles with uncountable nouns.

*I've always been interested in **big machinery**.*

*Thanks for **the information**.*

*He gave me **some really useful advice**.*

The definite article: *the*

We use *the*:

1 when we think it's clear which thing or things we mean.

*I read all **the comments from other gamers**.* (= the comments that other gamers make on my YouTube channel)

2 before some place names.

*I read recently about all these organised protests in **the United States**.*

*It was made in **the Philippines**.*

*We're going to **the Science Museum** tomorrow.*

*We sailed down **the Nile**.*

Note, however, that we don't use any articles before a lot of place names.

3 in some fixed expressions.

***In the end**, I stopped gaming.*

***By the way**, I don't live in my parents' basement.*

*I'm quite happy with what I've got **for the time being**.* (= from now to sometime in the future)

You just have to learn these expressions one by one, when you meet them.

We don't usually use any articles:

1 when we're using plural nouns to talk about things in general.

*I became obsessed with **roleplay games**.*

*It's taking money away from **designers** and **programmers**.*

2 after a preposition in a lot of expressions with places.

*I started gaming seriously when I was **at university**.*

*I almost completely stopped going **to class**.*

3 when we talk about continents, street names, parks, universities, restaurants, airports, stations and mountains.

Europe, Asia

Oxford Street. Fifth Avenue

Central Park, Hyde Park

Harvard, Beijing University of Technology

Noma, Central, Pujol

Heathrow, Narita, Schipol

Grand Central, Atocha, Victoria

Mount Everest, K2, Table Mountain

4 before the names of academic subjects, holidays, seasons or meals.

Law, History, Economics

Easter, Eid-al-Adha, Chinese New Year

Spring, Summer, Autumn, Winter

breakfast, lunch, dinner

Exercise 1

Choose the correct option.

1 *The technology / Technology / A technology* has completely changed the way people work.

2 *The technology / Technology / A technology* inside the camera is really clever.

3 My brother is *games designer / a games designer / the games designer*.

4 I've always been interested in *the computers / a computer / computers*.

5 *China / the China* is now the world leader in green technology.

6 I'll call you back later. I'm still *at work / at the work / at a work* at the moment.

7 *The man / A man / Man* who invented *Internet / an Internet / the Internet* is actually from *England / the England*.

8 *A main thing / Main thing / The main thing* I love about gaming is that it brings *people / a people / the people* together.

9 You probably don't know it, but it was *a very popular / very popular / the very popular* game when I was *a kid / the kid / kid*.

10 To tell *a truth / truth / the truth*, I used to be a bit of a gaming addict.

Exercise 2

Decide which six sentences are incorrect then correct them.

1 Very few of the people I know play computer games. Some don't even have mobiles!

2 I always hated the Science when I was at school.

3 I can't call you at the moment because I'm in the class.

4 The copper is an incredibly important metal used in computer manufacturing.

5 It's a shooter game. It's maybe the best thing I've ever played in my life.

6 He works for big computer company in Moscow.

7 I bought it when I was in United Arab Emirates for work last year.

8 I've always loved the gadgets.

INFINITIVE AND *-ING* FORMS

-ing forms as nouns

When we want to use a verb as a subject or object of a sentence, we use an *-ing* form.

***Having** something like that on your travels has to be good.*

*We didn't do **programming** in our IT classes at school.*

-ing forms after prepositions

When a verb follows a preposition, we use an *-ing* form.

*What's wrong **with using** your own voice?*

*We were all involved **in organising** the event.*

*I'm really looking forward **to going** to the gadget fair in San Francisco.*

-ing forms as adjectives

We can use some -ing forms as adjectives.

*What's more **embarrassing** ...*

*It's a very **exciting** development.*

-ing forms and continuous tenses

Remember we also use an -ing form to make continuous tenses.

*Someone's **following** you.* (present continuous)

*I **was talking** to him the other day and he said he'd bought a new car.* (past continuous)

*Have a rest. You**'ve been playing** that game for three hours!* (present perfect continuous)

Infinitive with *to* for purpose

We use an infinitive with *to* to explain the reason or purpose for doing something.

*You can use your phone **to lock** or unlock it from anywhere.*

*I need to go to the bank **to sort out** a problem.*

*I made a recording of my own music **to give** to friends.*

-ing form or infinitive with *to*?

Both -ing forms and infinitive with *to* can follow verbs with no preposition. There are no rules for which form goes after which verbs. It's just the way it is.

***Imagine walking** at night.* (imagine + -ing form)

*It's an app that **allows** you **to speak** in a foreign language.* (allow + object + infinitive with *to*)

Other verbs followed by an -ing form:

be caught	can't stand	fancy	feel like
keep	involve	mind	miss
recommend	risk	spend	suggest

Other verbs followed by an infinitive with *to*:

agree	arrange	ask	decide
deserve	fail	hope	intend
learn	manage	persuade	plan
promise	refuse	threaten	want

Exercise 1

Complete the sentences with the correct form of the verbs.

1 _____ computer games can be very educational. (play)

2 I was involved in _____ the website at work. (develop)

3 They should invent a robot _____ your pets while you're away. (look after)

4 The company finally agreed _____ me a refund for the faulty gadget. (give)

5 The app allows you _____ if any of your friends are nearby. (find out)

6 I can't stand people _____ with their smartphones while they're _____ to me. (mess around, talk)

7 I was thinking of _____ Computer Engineering there, but I failed _____ the grades I needed. (study, get)

8 You should get a cover for your phone _____ it _____ damaged. (prevent, get)

Exercise 2

Choose the correct option.

1 My job involves *travelling / to travel* a lot.

2 Do you fancy *going / to go* out somewhere this evening?

3 Sorry. I've arranged *meeting / to meet* a friend.

4 I'd rather stay in. I don't feel like *going / to go* out.

5 He played well. He didn't deserve *losing / to lose*.

6 I asked her very politely *emailing / to email* me a response, but I still haven't heard back from her.

7 I avoid *talking / to talk* to him as much as I can.

8 Unless you want to risk *losing / to lose* your work, you should set your computer to save automatically.

15 INJURIES AND ILLNESS

ADVERBS

Form

Most adverbs – but not all of them – are formed by adding -ly to an adjective. Adverbs ending with -ly often show the way we do something, or how much / how good. These adverbs are sometimes called adverbs of manner.

look **carefully**	walk **slowly**	shout **angrily**
wait **patiently**	produce it **naturally**	
absolutely fantastic	**incredibly** painful	
really hurt	**badly** sprain it	

Adverbs of frequency don't usually end in -ly.

always go	**often** find	**sometimes** wish
never need		

Some adverbs have the same form as an adverb and an adjective.

run **fast**	hit it **hard**	get up **early**
a **fast** runner	a **hard** exam	an **early** breakfast
arrive **late**	take **long**	
a **late** arrival	a **long** time	

Words with two adverb forms

Some adjectives have two adverb forms, e.g. *first / firstly, hard / hardly, late / lately*. Be careful – the two adverb forms often mean quite different things.

*He **works hard**.* (= He works a lot.)

*He **hardly sleeps**.* (= He doesn't sleep very much.)

*I **sleep late** most weekends.* (= I sleep till a late time.)

*I've been **sleeping badly lately**.* (= I've been sleeping badly recently.)

Position

A lot of adverbs can go in different positions in sentences. Use the following as a guide to what is generally correct.

Start of a sentence

Adverbs that show our opinion or attitude about what we're saying in the following part of the sentence usually go at the start of a sentence. These adverbs are sometimes called adverbs of attitude. They are followed by a comma.

***Hopefully**, it won't be more than half an hour.*

***Fortunately**, the hospital didn't charge us for the treatment.*

Other adverbs like this:

Amazingly   Apparently   Luckily   Personally   Sadly Unfortunately

Before the verb

Adverbs describing frequency or how much / how good usually go before the verb.

*I've **never** had any adverse reactions before.*

*I **really** enjoyed it.*

*It was **badly** sprained.*

After the verb

Adverbs showing how we did something tend to go after the verb.

*I listened **carefully**, but I didn't understand everything.*

*He works very **hard**.*

*Can you speak **more slowly**?*

End of a sentence

Adverbs showing when things happen often go at the end of a sentence (or clause).

I haven't been sleeping well **lately**.

I went to see a specialist **a few days ago**.

I have an appointment **tomorrow afternoon**.

Exercise 1

Put the adverbs in the most likely place in the sentences. You may need to change the punctuation.

1 I need to give you an injection, but you'll feel it. (hardly)

2 He's never had a day off work because of illness in 40 years. (amazingly)

3 I have been very tired. Maybe I'm getting a virus. (lately)

4 I was walking, but I still slipped. (quite carefully)

5 I broke it so I had to have an operation. (badly, unfortunately)

6 I was lucky I didn't hurt myself more. (really, seriously)

7 I wish I didn't have to get up, but usually I don't mind. (sometimes, early)

8 They can do the operation. You'll only be in the hospital for an afternoon. (these days, very quickly, apparently)

REPORTED SPEECH

When reporting things that have finished or which we believe to be untrue now, use past tenses. Reported speech usually moves one tense back from direct speech.

Present simple	➜ Past simple
Present continuous	➜ Past continuous
Present perfect simple	➜ Past perfect simple
Past simple	➜ Past perfect simple
be going to	➜ was going to
will	➜ would
can	➜ could
must / have to	➜ had to

'We**'ve given** him an X-ray and luckily nothing **is** broken.' (present perfect simple, present simple)

They rang and told me they**'d given** James an X-ray and there **was** nothing broken. (past perfect simple, past simple)

'He **needs** to stay here a bit longer, I'm afraid. He**'s waiting** to have a few stitches in the cuts.' (present simple, present continuous)

They said he **needed** to stay there a bit longer, though, as he **was waiting** to have a few stitches in the cuts. (past simple, past continuous)

'I**'ll take** him to the nearest hospital.' (will)

The woman driving said she**'d take** James to the nearest hospital. (would)

When what we are reporting is still true, we can use present and future forms in the normal way because we are talking from the point of view of now.

He said he**'s going to** have to buy a new bike now.

She said she **lives** in Madrid now.

They said they can't come tomorrow because they**'re working**.

Reporting questions

When we report questions, there is no inversion and we don't use do, does or did. As with reported statements, tenses usually go back if things have finished or are untrue now.

'Where am I? What happened?' (present simple, past simple)

He kept asking us **where he was** and **what had happened**. (past simple, past perfect simple)

When we report yes / no questions, we use if or whether.

'Have we met somewhere before?'

He even asked **if / whether we had met** somewhere before.

'Are you happy for me to have a look at it?'

She asked **if / whether she could have** a look at it.

Note that we can say either The doctor asked or The doctor asked me. It doesn't matter if we include the pronoun or not.

DID YOU KNOW?

Time and place words and pronouns often change when we report things people said.

'**I** saw him **yesterday**.'

She said **she**'d seen him **the day before** / **the previous day**.

'**We** can arrange an appointment for you **tomorrow**.'

They said I could come in and see a doctor **the next day** / **the following day**.

'Is there a hospital near **here**?'

He asked if there was a hospital near **there**.

Exercise 1

Complete the reported speech sentences below with the correct form of these verbs. You will need to add modal verbs in two sentences. Sometimes more than one answer is possible.

be	have	qualify	stop	suffer	take

1 A: He's suffering from stress.
   B: Really? That's strange. He told me he _____ from a heart condition.

2 A: She's having an operation to sort out the problem.
   B: I thought she said she _____ one already.

3 A: He's looking really well, isn't he?
   B: I know. It's amazing! The doctors told him it _____ him years to recover.

4 A: He's got his final exams next month.
   B: That's strange. I thought he said he _____ as a doctor already.

5 A: I feel guilty because we didn't help.
   B: You shouldn't. We did offer, but he said he _____ fine.

6 A: I just saw James outside – smoking again!
   B: Really? I thought he said he _____ the last time I spoke to him about it.

Exercise 2

Report the doctor's questions. If you think more than one answer is possible, write both options.

1 'Has anything like this happened before?'
   She asked me _____ .

2 'Does it hurt if I press here?'
   She asked _____ if she pressed on my arm.

3 'How do you think it happened?'
   She asked me _____ .

4 'Are you free to come in again next week?'
   She asked _____ .

5 'How did you manage to do that?'
   He asked me _____ it.

6 'Have you lost weight since the last time I saw you?'
   He asked _____ weight since the last time _____ me.

7 'Do you ever have problems sleeping?'
   He asked me _____ .

8 'Do you have any other questions you want to ask me?'
   He asked _____ .

16 NEWS AND EVENTS

REPORTING VERBS

Verb + clause

*She's just **announced** (that) they're splitting up.*

*The new management **claim** (that) it's too expensive to run.*

Other verbs like this are: *explain, say, state, reply, mention.*

Some verbs such as *tell* and *inform* need an object.

*He told **me** (that) he's getting divorced.*

verb + infinitive with *to*

*They even **promised to expand** last year.*

*No-one **offered to help**.*

*He's **refused to play** in any friendly matches.*

Other verbs like this are: *agree, ask, threaten, demand.*

Some verbs such as *advise, encourage, persuade, order, tell* and *warn* need an object.

*I warned **him** not to do it.*

*Apparently, they've persuaded **him** to stay.*

Verb + preposition + *-ing*

*He just **apologised for causing** the government difficulties.*

*Not that he's **admitted to doing** anything.*

*He's **been accused of doing** all kinds of things.*

Other verbs like this are: *complain about, insist on.*

These verbs can be followed by a noun instead of an *-ing* form.

*They apologised for **all the problems** we'd had.*

*I complained about **the service** at the hotel.*

Exercise 1

Choose the correct option.

1   The company finally agreed *to increase / they increase* the workers' wages.
2   The player was accused *to cheat / of cheating* to win the match.
3   The government is advising the public not *to travel / travelling* because of the bad weather.
4   The company has stated *not to know / it didn't know* about the problem until very recently.
5   Apparently, she threatened *to tell / she tell* the newspaper about their affair.
6   Before the election, the government promised *to lower / lowering* taxes, but they still haven't.
7   I'm not surprised you're ill. I did warn you *not to eat / not eating* the food at that place!
8   The police questioned him about the murder, but apparently he refused *to say / he said* anything.

Verbs with more than one pattern

Some verbs have more than one pattern.

*The company has **warned staff that they may** have to reduce the number of workers in the factory.* (verb + clause)

*The police **warned people not to gather** in the square to demonstrate.* (verb + infinitive with *to*)

*The government **insisted that its policy would work** eventually.* (verb + clause)

*After he was arrested, the man **insisted on his innocence**.* (verb + preposition + noun)

*He **insisted on paying** for everything, even though I offered to give him some money.* (verb + preposition + *-ing*)

Exercise 2

Complete the second sentence so that it has a similar meaning to the first sentence using the word given. Do not change the word given. You must use between three and five words, including the word given.

1   He said he was sorry he was late.
    APOLOGISED
    He _____ late.
2   His exact words were, 'If you tell anyone about this, you're fired!'
    THREATENED
    He _____ I told anyone about it.
3   She said there was absolutely no way she was signing the contract.
    REFUSED
    She simply _____ the contract.
4   She said I would be good and I should apply for the job.
    ENCOURAGED
    She _____ the job.
5   They warned me not to go out at night on my own.
    SHOULDN'T
    They said _____ on my own at night.
6   He told me he would definitely pay me tomorrow.
    TO
    He _____ me tomorrow.

DEFINING RELATIVE CLAUSES

We use relative clauses to add information after nouns. We use different relative pronouns (*who, which, that,* etc.) in clauses depending on the nouns we are adding information to or on the information that follows.

To add information about people, we use a clause beginning with *that* or *who*.

*She's the woman **that spoke to me earlier**.*

*Roentgen was the scientist **who discovered radiation**.*

To add information about things, we use a clause beginning with *that* or *which*.

*She wrote a book **that was a huge best-seller**.*

*It's a government scheme **which helps unemployed people**.*

To add information about times, we use a clause beginning with *when* or *that*.

*I remember the day **when Princess Diana died** very clearly.*

*At the time **that he was writing**, there was a war going on.*

*That's **when I realised I'd made a mistake**.*

To add information about possessions, we use a clause beginning with *whose*.

*That's the couple **whose child went missing last year**.*

*He made a film **whose main character becomes the US President by accident**.*

To add information about places, we use a clause beginning with *where*.

*That's the hospital **where I was born**!*

*What's the name of that bar **where you went for your birthday**?*

DID YOU KNOW?

When adding information about places, we can replace *where* with *that / which* + preposition.

*That's the hospital **that / which I was born in**.*

*What's the name of that bar **that / which you went to for your birthday**?*

Exercise 1

Match the beginnings of sentences 1–6 with the pairs of relative clauses a–f.

1 Did you apply for that job
2 Did you read about that guy
3 What's the name of that company
4 We met that woman
5 We went to that bar
6 He's the writer

a that you recommended. It was really good!
   where all the stars go, but we didn't see anyone famous!
b which went bankrupt last week?
   that Maria works for?
c whose novel was banned by the government.
   who won the Nobel prize a couple of years ago.
d that you were telling me about?
   which was advertised in the paper yesterday?
e who works with you. I've forgotten her name!
   that you said you're interested in.
f who they arrested for that big robbery?
   that was awarded the Nobel peace prize?

Exercise 2

Complete the film review with appropriate relative pronouns.

Lorenzo's Oil is a film [1]_____ tells the true story of a couple [2]_____ child develops medical problems at the age of seven. The first doctors [3]_____ see him have no idea what is causing the problem, but he is eventually diagnosed with a disease [4]_____ is called ALD and is incurable. They ask about hospitals [5]_____ they are doing research on this disease, but they are told it is so rare that no-one will pay the money [6]_____ is needed to investigate it. The couple, who have no medical training, then start to study medical literature to find something [7]_____ will help their son. I love this film because at the time [8]_____ I saw it, I was also quite ill, and it was very uplifting. Like the boy in the film, I eventually got better.

INFORMATION FILES

FILE 11

Unit 13 page 49   GRAMMAR

Situation 1

You checked in for a flight and went to have something to eat. When you went to the departure lounge, there was a queue to transfer to the terminal and extra security. When you walked up to the boarding gate, the airline said it was closed and they would charge you for a new ticket.

Situation 2

You hired a car. You got a flat tyre and there wasn't a spare one so you called roadside assistance. Just before you took the car back, you filled the tank with the wrong kind of petrol. Now the car company wants to charge you for both problems and you don't have any insurance.

Situation 3

You reserved a seat on a train to attend an important meeting. The first train arrived five minutes late so you missed the connection. The next train was full and you had to stand for two hours. You arrived at the meeting tired, late and angry and it went badly. Now you want compensation from the train operator.

Situation 4

You and a friend hired a car to go to a wedding. Your friend had been to the place before so said you didn't need a GPS. You left the motorway to avoid a traffic jam and then got completely lost. When you got back on the motorway, you tried to make up for lost time, but were caught speeding and now you have to pay a fine. You think your friend should pay it.

FILE 16

1 squirrel

2 lizard

3 bear

4 eagle

5 dolphin

6 cockroach

7 deer

8 whale

9 wolf

10 crow

11 crocodile

12 parrot

13 snake

14 scorpion

15 rat

AUDIO SCRIPTS

▶ TRACK 41

G = Gavin, L = Lynn

G: Did I tell you I went round to see Nick and Carol the other day?

L: No, you didn't. How are they? I haven't seen them for ages.

G: Oh, they're fine. They said to say 'hello' to you. You know they've moved recently, don't you?

L: Oh really? No, I didn't, actually. The last time I heard from them they were still in that place near the centre.

G: Oh, OK. Well, yeah, they've moved, um … I think it was last month. To be honest, they seem much happier now.

L: Oh, that's good. So what's their new place like? Is it nice?

G: Yeah, it is. It's OK. It's quite a lot bigger than their old place. The front room is huge – it's about twice the size of this room – and the whole place is pretty spacious.

L: That must be nice for them now the kids are growing up.

G: I know. They said the old place was getting a bit cramped for them all. They wanted separate rooms for the kids. They didn't want them sharing forever! That's the main reason they moved out.

L: So what kind of place is it? I mean, is it a house or an apartment?

G: Oh, it's an apartment. It's on the third floor of an old block. It's a little bit run-down and they'll need to do quite a bit of work on it, but they've actually bought it, so they can do what they want to it.

L: Lucky them! All those weekends spent painting and decorating to look forward to!

G: I know! I don't envy them! It has got real potential, though. It's got a great kitchen – it's a similar size to yours, maybe a bit bigger – and it's got these lovely old wooden floors throughout. And huge windows, so they get a lot of sunlight coming in, which is great. Then there's a little balcony where you can sit and eat in the summer and a shared garden out the back where the kids can play, and everything.

L: Oh, it sounds lovely. I must go round and see them sometime soon.

G: Yeah, I'm sure they'd like that. The only problem is, though, it's not as central as their old place was. It's quite a lot further out, so it takes quite a long time to get there.

L: Oh, OK.

▶ TRACK 42

1 the other day
2 to be honest
3 the only problem is
4 in the attic
5 on the eighth floor
6 Where's the exit?

▶ TRACK 43

S = Shola, A = Anastasia

A: Are you Shola?

S: Yeah. Anastasia?

A: Yes. Nice to meet you.

S: You too.

A: You found the right stop then?

S: Yeah, yeah. It was all very easy. Is the flat near here then?

A: Yes, it's just down this side street. I just thought it was easier to meet here.

S: No, sure. It's very convenient to get around then. I didn't realise it was quite so central.

A: Of course. I guess that's why it's more popular than it used to be.

S: Right. What's happening there then?!

A: I don't know. Maybe just an accident.

S: Really? Because I saw a burnt car on my way here – it seems a bit rough.

A: No. It's true it was a bit dangerous before, but the authorities did a lot and there's much less crime now. I mean, of course there can be trouble now, but it was so much worse in the past.

S: The graffiti's kind of cool.

A: It is cool. And of course we have the park and the river.

S: Yeah?

A: You like running?

S: Not really.

A: Well, it's good for sunbathing then.

S: A bit chilly for that.

A: In the summer, though … you can go naked!

S: Er … OK.

A: So, here we are.

S: Nice building.

A: Much better now it's restored. It was falling down before my parents bought the place. It had … I think you call them … um, squatters? You see all this staircase? It's all been restored.

S: So your parents bought it? You mean, the whole building?

A: Yeah, it was an investment a few years ago. Property prices have gone up a lot now.

S: Right.

A: So, we're on the top floor.

S: Wait, there's no lift?

A: No, it's not possible.

A: Almost there! OK, you're here!

S: Oh! I'm not as fit as I used to be! I guess you must be used to it, though.

A: Yeah, I'm much thinner than I was. I've lost 30 kilos!

S: Really?

A: No, I'm joking. But it keeps you fit. So come in. Here's the living room. We share.

S: OK. Nice. Oh, great view.

A: Yes. And this would be your room.

S: OK. It's a bit smaller than I expected.

A: Really? I had another English man here who said it was 'cosy'!

S: That's one word. But not much space if I wanted a friend to visit. Can I have visitors?

A: I'm afraid not. I want you to myself. Ha, ha. I'm joking, of course. It is very small I think with visitors, but I can recommend some places nearby.

S: OK. Well, the kitchen's nice and big. Is it OK if I cook here whenever I like?

A: Sure – as long as I'm not preparing something.

S: Right – that might be awkward.

A: But there's a microwave. You can do microwave meals.

S: Hmm. Hey, nice speakers! You like music, yeah? Would you mind if I played my music in here?

A: Within reason. Obviously you can't play rap.

S: Well, that's OK. I'm not really into …

A: I'm joking! Of course I love rap!

S: OK … well … rap's OK. You know, I think I've seen enough.

A: I'll show you the toilet.

S: I have a couple of other places to see. So I'd better get going.

A: OK, well ring me when you've decided.

S: Sure.

▶ TRACK 44

1

A: Would it be OK if I have friends to visit?

B: It depends how long for. It's fine if it's just a few days.

2

A: Would you mind if I cooked for myself sometimes?

B: Not at all – as long as you clean up after yourself.

3

A: Do I have to be home before a certain time?

B: No, not at all – as long as you're quiet if you're back late.

4

A: Can I use the washing machine whenever I like?

B: Within reason. Obviously, I don't want you washing clothes in the middle of the night!

5

A: Would it be possible to move a table into my room?

B: I'm afraid not, no. The two we have are needed downstairs.

6

A: Is it OK if I play music in my room?

B: Of course, within reason. Obviously, you shouldn't play it too loud.

UNIT 10

▶ TRACK 45

D = Dan, J = Jason

D: Do you fancy going out later?

J: Yeah, maybe. What's on?

D: Well, do you like horror films?

J: Yeah, if I'm in the right mood. Why?

D: Well, there's this Brazilian film on in town that I'd quite like to see. It's got English subtitles, so it should be OK.

J: Oh right. So what's it about, then? What's the plot?

D: Well, apparently, it's about zombies taking over Brasília.

J: That sounds fun.

D: Yeah and the special effects are supposed to be amazing as well.

J: Cool. So when's it on?

D: There's a showing at just after nine and then a late one at twelve.

J: OK. Well, I'm not sure I want to go to the late one. I need to be up quite early tomorrow.

D: That's OK. The ten past nine showing is good for me.

J: Where's it on?

D: The Capitol.

J: OK then. Great.

▶ TRACK 46

D = Dan, J = Jason

D: So do you know where the cinema is?

J: I think so. Isn't The Capitol that one near the river?

D: Nope. That's the ABC.

J: Oh right. Well in that case, no, I'm not sure.

D: The Capitol's in the centre – on Crown Street.

J: OK. I don't know it, then.

D: You know Oxford Road, yeah? Well, that's the main street which goes past the railway station.

J: Yeah, yeah.

D: Well, if you have your back to the station, you turn right down Oxford Road. You walk about 200 metres and you go past a post office.

J: OK.

D: And the next street after that is Crown Street. The cinema's along there, about halfway down on the left.

J: Oh yeah. I think I know the place now. There's a big sweet shop right opposite, isn't there?

D: That's the one.

J: OK. So if the programme starts at ten past nine, what time do you want to meet? Shall I just meet you on the steps outside at nine?

D: Can we make it eight thirty? We want to be sure we get a ticket.

J: I doubt it'll be that busy, but I suppose we could get there a bit earlier. We can always get a coffee before the film starts.

D: Exactly. Maybe whoever gets there first should start queuing, OK?

J: OK, but I don't think we need to worry. I don't think that many people will want to see a Brazilian zombie movie.

D: Hey, you never know!

▶ TRACK 47

1 You know Columbus Avenue? Well, the restaurant's about halfway down there.

2 The bus stop is right in front of the main entrance to the station.

3 You know the post office? Well, St Ann's Road is the next turning down from there, on the other side of the road.

4 You know the cinema? Well, there's a car park at the back.

5 You know the main square? Well, Hope Close is one of the streets off there.

6 If you have your back to the station, you turn left.

7 If you're facing the station, the shop will be on your right.

8 If you're coming down the road away from the station, Church Street's the second turning on the left.

9 If you're going up the road towards the station and away from the river, Pemberton Road's the second on the right.

10 When you come out of the building, you'll see the cinema right opposite.

1

A: So how was it?

B: Oh, it was brilliant – much better than I thought it'd be.

A: Really? I'd heard it wasn't that good.

B: Well, me too, but I actually really enjoyed it.

A: So, what's so good about it?

B: Oh, the story, the acting – everything. It's just really funny and it's quite exciting too. I don't know. Maybe it's because I didn't think it'd be anything special.

A: I know what you mean. You see so many films these days where there's so much advance publicity – especially from Hollywood. It's all in the papers and everyone's saying, 'You have to go and see it.' And then you go and you just end up thinking it was a bit overrated. It's nice to go to something that actually meets your expectations.

2

C: Did you have a good night out? How was the concert?

D: Oh, we didn't go in the end.

C: Really? What a shame.

D: I know! Hans was going to pick me up at seven, but as it happened he had to finish some work at the office and by the time we got there, there was a massive queue for tickets. So we decided we weren't going to get in and we went to a club instead.

C: Oh right. So what club did you go to?

D: Radio City.

C: Well, that's supposed to be really good. It's quite trendy, isn't it?

D: That's what they say, but I hated it!

C: Really? What was so bad about it?

D: It was just awful – the people, the music, everything. It's one of the worst clubs I've ever been to.

C: Really?

D: OK, maybe I'm exaggerating a bit. I mean, it was OK to begin with, but then it got absolutely packed, so you couldn't really dance properly. And it was boiling hot, so you were sweating like crazy. And then they changed the music later to this heavy techno stuff, which I hate. And the drinks were a rip-off.

C Oh dear. Maybe you just went on the wrong night.

3

E: I'm so tired! I was out late last night.

F: Really? I thought you said you were going to have a quiet night in.

E: I know. I mean, I was going to stay in, but Clara phoned and while we were chatting, she mentioned she had a spare ticket for this play in town and so I said I'd go with her.

F: Oh right. So what did you go and see? Anything good?

E: Yes, actually. It was called *A Man for All Seasons*.

F: Oh! I've been wanting to see that for ages! It's had some great reviews in the papers. How was it?

E: Brilliant! One of the best things I've seen in a long time.

F: That's what I'd heard.

E: Yeah. It's so moving. Honestly, I was in tears at the end. And the whole staging – the lighting, the costumes, everything – it's just really well done.

F: I'll have to go.

E: Yeah, you should.

1 I said I'd do it and I will.

2 I said I wouldn't, but in the end I did.

3 The divorce rate has risen dramatically over recent years.

4 There's been a steady fall in unemployment.

5 Much was said, but little was done.

6 There's not as much crime as there was in the past.

1

A: That's a nice photo. Who's that?

B: Oh, it's a friend.

A: And is that your cat?

B: Yeah.

A: It's so cute!

B: I know. Mind you she's lucky she's still alive!

A: Really? What happened?

B: Well, when she was a little kitten she actually got stuck inside the wall of our house!

A: You're joking! How did that happen?

B: We're not absolutely sure, because we didn't see her disappear, but we think she crawled through a little hole in the floor in our bedroom and then she fell down the gap between the walls.

A: Oh no.

B: Anyway, we were watching TV and we could hear these little cries coming from somewhere, but we were going mad because we couldn't see her anywhere and then we worked out she was actually inside the wall!

A: So how did you get her out?

B: We had to call the fire service in the end, and they basically broke a bit of the outside wall and they managed to get her out like that. Here, I think I still have a picture …

A: Oh, look at that! Oh that sad little face!

B: I know. I'm glad we found her.

2

C: You'll never guess what happened last night.

D: Go on. What?

C: Well, I was writing some reports on my computer at home when I suddenly noticed a group of crows looking quite excited. They were all making this dreadful noise so I went outside to see what was happening.

D: And?

C: Well, the crows were chasing a little parrot up and down the street.

D: A parrot? What was it doing there?

C: I have no idea. I guess it must've escaped from somewhere. Anyway, it was obviously very scared and cold. I felt really sorry for it so I chased the crows away. The parrot was then sitting on my neighbour's roof and I didn't want to leave it.

D: Yeah? So what happened in the end? Did you catch it?

C: Yeah, I had to put some fruit and seeds on the ground to tempt it down and then when it came down, I managed to catch it and put it into a box. We've got it at home now.

D: Wow! That's mad. Actually, it reminds me of something I saw a few weeks ago. I was coming home from work on my bicycle when …

3

E: I really thought I was going to die. Honestly, I hope I never see another crocodile in my life!

F: I can imagine. That's awful! It actually reminds me of something that happened to me last year in Indonesia.

E: Oh yeah? What was that?

F: Well, I was there on holiday, and I'd decided to spend a few days trekking through the jungle. On the second day, we were walking along a path through the rainforest when suddenly these huge lizards came running out of the bushes from all sides. They were enormous – much bigger than me! Everyone ran away, leaving me with three of these monster lizards running towards me. I tried to scream, but just couldn't! I really thought they were going to eat me.

E: Really? That sounds terrifying! So what happened?

F: Well, luckily, the guides managed to stop the lizards with these big sticks they had, and so I managed to escape.

▶ TRACK 51

1 Oh, they're <u>so</u> cute!
2 He's <u>so</u> lovely.
3 He's <u>so</u> annoying!
4 Their dog is just <u>rea</u>lly out of control!
5 It smells <u>rea</u>lly bad.
6 It's just in<u>cre</u>dibly noisy!
7 He <u>e</u>ven lets the cat walk on the table.
8 He <u>ac</u>tually kisses the dog and lets it lick his face!

▶ TRACK 52

1

A: You'll never guess what happened last night.

B: Go on. What?

A: Well, I was walking home when I suddenly saw a horse, standing there in the street!

2

C: I saw something really strange while we were away.

D: Oh yeah? What was that?

C: We saw this whale stuck on the beach.

D: Seriously? Still alive?

C: Yeah! It was actually quite upsetting! We phoned the police to see if they could organise help.

3

E: I was just about to put my shoes on when I found a scorpion hiding in one of the shoes!

F: Really? What was that doing there?

E: I don't know. I guess it was just looking for somewhere to sleep.

4

G: We spent hours trying to persuade the cat to come down from the tree, but it refused to come.

H: Oh no! That's awful! So what happened in the end?

G: Well, eventually, we gave up. But an hour later it walked into the kitchen, looking for its dinner!

▶ TRACK 53

Obviously Wilson's story is a tragedy. He had no real idea of the power of nature and he died because of it. But I don't think he was stupid. Remember his terrible experience in the war. That can affect people in different ways, and maybe those terrible memories are what drove him. Then think about his achievement. Just reaching Everest was really amazing. All those difficulties he overcame: the flight to India, the walk, everything. And he showed skill in learning to fly and amazing strength and determination – and he did it alone. That's so different to these people who pay to go up Everest. They arrive in helicopters. They carry almost nothing and they're not just risking their own lives, they risk many lives. If a rope broke, how many people would fall? If a guide got injured, these amateurs couldn't help. And with so many of them, serious climbers have to wait in these really dangerous conditions. And if that wasn't bad enough, they leave so much rubbish on the mountain – broken tents, ropes, empty oxygen bottles – things that stay there forever in the freezing cold.

▶ TRACK 54

Now, you might think that countries and regions that are rich in natural resources, such as coal or oil, would have the strongest economies. In fact, though, they often suffer from something called 'the resource curse'. How many of you have heard of this before? OK, a couple of you. Well, this phrase was first used in the 1990s by the writer Richard Auty, who argued that having lots of natural resources actually causes problems for the economy. Since then, his theory has been supported by several studies that have found that, yes, there are rich people in these countries, but, on average, the typical person in resource-rich countries is less wealthy than in countries with few natural resources. The question is, why? What's happening? Well, I'm going to suggest four main reasons: conflict, corruption, value of manufactured products and instability.

So, conflict. Where there are natural resources, there is big money to be made. But where there's big money, there's often big trouble and a fight for control. Local people are often forced to leave their land so that resources can be extracted, and that causes controversy. The anger may be worse because they receive no money for moving and the profits from the extraction go to foreign companies or other parts of the country. Regions with large reserves may try to gain independence from the rest of the country so that they can control the natural resource. The result can be violent protests, even civil war. And you don't need me to tell you how oil has also caused expensive international wars.

Then there's corruption. Profits from mining and drilling often go to politicians and officials, rather than helping to build schools or hospitals for local people. Companies may give 'presents' to officials to avoid expensive rules and regulations – I'm sure you know what I mean. Politicians may directly run a mining company or be employed by them on huge 'salaries'.

Thirdly, the basic materials, like oil or wood, are not as valuable as manufactured products made from them, like petrol or furniture. So if you are a country with few resources, you have to do something else. So you invest in manufacturing and then these economies grow quicker than the countries which mainly produce natural resources.

Why don't resource-rich countries invest in factories? Well, largely because of corruption and conflict, but it's also because economic instability can reduce investment. Global prices of natural resources vary a lot. If the price falls suddenly, there is obviously crisis. But big price rises are also bad. When resource prices go up, the country's currency also rises. If the currency is high, factories can't sell their products because imports are cheap and exporting is expensive. These risks mean less investment is made, which then makes the economy depend more on the natural resource, which is why it's called a 'resource curse'!

▶ TRACK 55

Not every country rich in resources has suffered though. A few have managed to become successful and one of the best examples is the African state of Botswana. The country gained independence from Britain in 1966. It was then one of the world's poorest countries, but, one year later, diamonds were discovered in the Kalahari Desert. In 1969, the government made an agreement with the South African company De Beers, and today around a quarter of all the world's diamonds are mined there. For over 40 years now, profits have been invested in health care, education and infrastructure, such as roads. This investment has made the big difference, but it could only happen because there's a strong democracy and good government, which according to Transparency International has the lowest level of corruption in Africa.

UNIT 12

▶ TRACK 56

cre<u>a</u>tive	<u>sen</u>sitive	am<u>bi</u>tious	di<u>rect</u>
in<u>tense</u>	<u>bright</u>	<u>charm</u>ing	diplo<u>mat</u>ic
<u>loy</u>al	<u>calm</u>	com<u>pet</u>itive	<u>mod</u>est

▶ TRACK 57

L = Lewis, J = Jessica

L: Where did you disappear to?

J: Yeah, sorry. I had to go and phone my brother, Noel. It's his birthday today.

L: Oh, OK. It's just that you were quite a long time.

J: I know. I was only going to be five minutes – just wish him 'Happy Birthday' – but once he starts talking, he doesn't stop!

L: Oh, that's like my mum. She can talk for hours. I sometimes think we could be on the phone and I could go off and have a coffee and then come back and she'd still be talking! She wouldn't have noticed I'd gone!

J: Right. Well, I'm not sure he's quite that bad.

L: OK, maybe I'm exaggerating, but she is very talkative. Anyway, it sounds like you and Noel get on well.

J: Yeah, really well. Unfortunately I don't see him that much now because he's living in the States.

L: Really! What's he doing there? Is he working?

J: No, he won a scholarship to study Physics.

L: Wow! He must be clever.

J: He is. He's really bright – always top of his class. But, you know, he's not one of those intense clever people. He's really funny and very good with people.

L: Sounds a great guy. Do you have any other brothers or sisters? I don't think you've told me before.

J: Maybe not. Er I've got a younger brother called Greg.

L: And what's he like? Do you get on well?

J: Yeah, I guess.

L: You don't sound too sure.

J: No. I mean, he's nice and everything. We're just ... different.

L: Yeah? In what way?

J: I don't know. He's just so sensitive. I seem to upset him a lot, anyway.

L: Oh yeah?

J: Yeah, for example, he wants to be an artist, yeah?

L: Oh right.

J: And the other week I saw him at my mum and dad's and he was talking about his big new art project – some kind of installation.

L: Right.

J: And I asked, 'So where and when is this going to be on?', and he just got annoyed and went quiet.

L: Oh?

J: Basically, because it won't happen. He likes the idea of being creative, but he doesn't want to do the work. I've told him before: you need to be ambitious, push yourself more, or you'll never make any money.

L: Oh ... right.

J: What?

L: No, you're right. It's tough being an artist. It's just that ...

J: What?

L: Well ... I guess you get plenty of criticism in the art world and maybe he doesn't want his sister to be so direct?

J: Oh, right. So you think it's my fault!

L: No! I'm just saying ...

J: Whatever.

L: It's ... hard ... so, are we going for coffee?

J: I guess.

▶ TRACK 58

1   Doug

I met him while doing a summer job in England. We were both working in this café – he was in the kitchens and I was a waiter. Our boss was a bit of an idiot. He was really strict – he was always shouting at us and was just horrible. Anyway, we used to go out after work and we'd sit and complain about our boss. We'd talk about the things we wished we'd said to him. Nicolas was always very funny about it.

2   Sandra

We were dating for a while. I met him when we were studying in Rome on an Erasmus programme. It was a great few months. He was always so much fun and so full of life. We tried to keep the relationship going after he went back to Belgium, but it's difficult maintaining a long-distance relationship. We couldn't afford to visit each other very often and, in the end, we split up. We've remained friends, which I suppose is important, but I sometimes wish we'd stayed together. Yeah, I wish we hadn't split up.

3   Shane

I met him while I was backpacking. We were staying in a hostel and we had to share a room. We got talking and found we had a lot in common. We ended up spending a couple of weeks sightseeing until I went back to Australia. We kept in touch via email and social media after that and two years ago I moved to Britain. Since then, I've been over to Belgium to see him a couple of times.

4   Brigitta

We met at university. We didn't have much to do with each other at first as we're so different. I think I'm quite sociable and outgoing and, as you probably know, he's a bit quiet and shy. It's not that we didn't get on at all. We'd see each other in class and in the library and we'd chat a bit. Over time, though, our chats got longer, and then, just before we left university, I asked him out on a date. He looked a bit surprised, but he said OK and we've been seeing each other now for about two years. It's a shame it took so long for us to get together, really!

5   Franck

I met him through a friend, Jef, who he was sharing a flat with. We all used to hang out together so I'd talk to Nicolas and got to know him very well. At some point I had an argument with Jef. It was about something stupid, but we basically stopped talking to each other. We're both very stubborn and I didn't want to be the first to apologise, but of course, neither did he! I regret that, really. I wish we'd managed to sort things out between us, but … there you go. Anyway, to cut a long story short, I haven't seen Jef for years, but I'm still friends with Nicolas.

▶ TRACK 59

1   I wish I'd known.
2   I wish I'd met him.
3   I wish they'd told me earlier.
4   I wish I'd tried harder at school.
5   I really wish we hadn't moved house.
6   Honestly, I wish I hadn't said anything.
7   I wish I hadn't gone to the meeting.
8   I sometimes wish they'd given me a different name.

REVIEW 6

▶ TRACK 60

1   I used to, but I don't anymore.
2   I tried it, but I really wish I hadn't.
3   I'd go there all the time when I was a kid.
4   They found it again two days after it'd been stolen.
5   I could see it from the hotel, but didn't manage to visit.
6   We couldn't use the pool because it was being cleaned.

UNIT 13

▶ TRACK 61

1

M = Maria, B = Belinda, A = Andre

M: Thanks for picking us up. It's really kind of you.
B: That's OK. It's no problem. So, how was your journey?
M: Oh, quite stressful, actually. It's a relief to finally be here.
B: Oh no! What happened? You weren't delayed or anything, were you?
M: No, no, it wasn't that, thank goodness, but everything else that could go wrong did! To begin with, we almost missed the flight, because Andre didn't want to spend too long hanging around at the airport.
A: I've already said I'm sorry!
M: He said we'd be OK if we got there an hour and a half before take-off, but there was a huge queue at the check-in desk and then another one going through security, so in the end we only just caught the flight.
B: How come it was so busy? It's not really the holiday season.

A: Exactly. They were doing extra security checks for some reason.
B: Oh right.
M: Whatever, if we'd been there earlier …
A: OK, OK.
M: Anyway, the flight was dreadful too.
A: Awful. We hit a big storm coming over France and it was so bumpy …
M: Honestly, at one point, I thought we were going to crash!
A: I was sweating!
B: That sounds terrifying.
M: It was! I don't want to go through that again, I can tell you!
A: Me neither.
B: I'm sure. What do you want to do now? Do you want to go and get something to eat, or do you want to check in at the hotel first?

2

L = Lara, K = Karen

L: Hi. There you are! I was starting to worry.
K: Yeah, sorry I'm so late. I had a bit of a nightmare getting here.
L: Oh really? How come?
K: Well, to begin with, it was still dark when I set off.
L: Really? What time did you leave?
K: Six. And then it immediately started to pour down, so the roads were really slippery.
L: Oh, I hate driving in the rain – especially in the dark.
K: So do I. That's probably why I took a wrong turning. I got completely lost and ended up going round in circles for ages. I couldn't work out where I was or where I was going! Then, when I finally got back onto the right road, I almost had an accident.
L: Seriously? What happened?
K: Oh, it wasn't anything bad. It was just this stupid guy in a big expensive car who drove straight across me. I had to brake to avoid hitting him. I wasn't hurt or anything, but I did have to stop and park the car for a few minutes to calm down.
L: Oh, you poor thing. That's awful – but that's male drivers for you!

▶ TRACK 62

1

A: What was the weather like in Peru? Was it hot?
B: No, it wasn't, actually. We arrived at night and it was freezing. Then during the day it was still chilly and cloudy.
A: Oh dear.
B: I wish I'd taken some warmer clothes. I only had T-shirts and one thin jacket.
A: Oh no!
B: It was stupid. I should've thought more carefully before setting off. I knew we'd be in the mountains and could've checked the forecast.
A: I guess, but South America – you assume it'll be hot.
B: Exactly! It's silly, really! Anyway, we still had an amazing time!

2

D: Hello.
C: Hello, Mum. It's me, Alan.
D: Oh hello. I was worried. Did you arrive safely?
C: Yeah, sorry, we got here late – that's why I didn't phone.
D: Oh right. So, is everything OK? Are you both well?
C: Yeah, fine, except for the cockroaches in the hotel.
D: Cockroaches!
C: Yeah. We stayed in this little place last night and the room was filthy.

D: That's horrible!

C: We were silly. We should've looked around more, but because we got here so late, we just chose the first cheap place we came across.

D: Oh Alan!

C: Don't worry – we'll check the place out better next time.

D: I hope so.

3

E: How was Greece? Nice and hot?

F: Yes, it was. It was boiling!

E: Lucky you! I bet that was nice.

F: It was, but I did get sunburnt on the first day.

E: Oh no!

F: It was really hot and I was sunbathing and just fell asleep. The next day, my skin went purple! It was horrible.

E: Oh you poor thing!

F: Oh, it was my own fault. I shouldn't have stayed in the sun for so long, especially with my skin. I should've at least put on some sun cream!

4

G: Hello Sir. Are all three of you flying together to Prague?

H: Yes, that's right.

G: In that case, I'll just need to weigh your bags.

H: Sure.

G: I'm afraid you have to pay an excess baggage charge of €100 on this bag.

H: What? But there are three of us! The baggage allowance is fifteen kilos each.

G: I'm sorry Sir, but the rules are very clear: the maximum for any one bag is fifteen kilos, and this one weighs 25. You can transfer some weight to your hand baggage if you like.

H: How can we fit ten kilos in there? It's tiny!

G: Well, in that case you need to pay the excess.

H: That's ridiculous.

G: I'm sorry, but it really isn't my fault. The ticket conditions are very clear. I'm afraid you have to go back to the desk over there and pay the excess.

H: But the queue's huge!

I: I told you we should've brought another suitcase.

H: I just thought it would be easier with two.

I: €100! That's such a rip-off!

1

A: How did you find the museum? It was absolutely <u>packed</u> when we went!

B: It was busy, but it wasn't too crowded.

2

A: You must be angry they've lost your luggage.

B: Yeah, I am. I'm absolutely <u>furious</u>!

3

A: You must be ex<u>hau</u>sted after such a long journey.

B: I am a bit tired but I actually slept on the plane for a while.

4

A: You must be hungry after such a long journey.

B: I am. I'm absolutely <u>star</u>ving. Have you got anything to eat?

5

A: How was the journey back? Did you get wet in that storm?

B: We got absolutely <u>soaked</u>! I didn't have an umbrella or anything.

6

A: Did you like the food? I thought it was absolutely de<u>li</u>cious.

B: Yeah, it was quite tasty, but I've had better.

7

A: The place we stayed in was a bit dirty.

B: A bit? It was absolutely <u>fil</u>thy! I couldn't believe it.

8

A: I've heard Tabriz is a very interesting city.

B: Yeah, it is. It's <u>fas</u>cinating. It has so much history!

UNIT 14

1

A: Hello. Help desk.

B: Yeah. Hi there. I wonder if you can help me. I've just turned on my computer and found that the Internet's down.

A: What? No! All of it? That's a disaster!

B: What?

A: Oh, nothing. Just my little joke. Have you checked all the connections? Maybe something's not plugged in properly?

B: I think everything's OK, yes. One minute. Let me just have one more look … yep … I've just checked all the plugs and sockets again, but it hasn't made any difference.

A: Hmm. Well, in that case, there's probably an issue with the cable then. I'll come down and have a look in a bit, OK?

2

A: Hello. IT.

C: Hi. I've got a bit of a problem. My computer crashed this morning and when I turned it back on all the folders I keep my files in had disappeared from the screen.

A: OK. Well, you must have backup copies somewhere, right? On an external hard drive or in the Cloud?

C: I'm afraid not. It's stupid of me, I know, but I always forget to copy them.

A: Right. Well, in future, you might want to think about backing up more often. Have you tried rebooting at all?

C: Um … what does that mean?

A: Turning it off and turning it on again.

C: Oh, OK. I need these things in plain English, you see! But yes, I have and it didn't do any good.

A: OK. Have you tried searching for specific files by name?

C: No, not yet. Should I?

A: Yeah, try that and see if anything comes up.

3

A: Hello Help desk.

D: Hi there. I've got a bit of problem down in accounts. I'm trying to print some files and every time I go to select 'print' from the drop-down menu, my cursor just turns into that spinning wheel of death thing, you know, that circle that just goes round and round and round. I move it away with the mouse and it stops and goes back to normal. Honestly, it's driving me mad!

A: OK. That's a very specific problem. I'm not sure I've dealt with anything like that before. I think you may have got a virus. Have you run a security scan?

D: No, I haven't, but I could if you think it'll help.

A: Yeah, try that and see what happens. It should find any unwanted software that's hiding away in there and it'll give you greater protection in future if you need it as well.

D: OK.

A: Otherwise, let me Google it and see what I can find.

4

A: Hello, IT Help desk.

E: Hi Bob. It's me, Martin again, I'm afraid.

A: Let me guess. Password problems?

E: Yes. Sorry. I'm just hopeless at remembering these things! What is it now? Three times this month.

A: At least. But don't worry. You're not the worst offender.

E: It's the age we live in! I've got more passwords than I have friends!

A: I'll reset it for you and email you a new one in a minute, OK?

E: Thanks.

A: Have you tried that app, by the way? I think it's called 'All My Passwords'.

E: No.

A: Well, try that. It might help. Otherwise, you might need to get some more memory installed.

▶ TRACK 65

1 Have you tried downloading it?
2 Yeah, but I didn't have any success.
3 Maybe you should tell her.
4 OK. I'll try that.
5 Otherwise, I don't know what else to suggest.
6 I've tried, but it didn't make any difference.
7 OK. Well, have you looked on the Internet?
8 No, not yet. Do you think I should?
9 Otherwise, you're probably best doing an actual course somewhere.

▶ TRACK 66

The computer and video games industry has experienced remarkable growth. Worth around $25 billion around a decade ago, interactive entertainment now generates well over $100 billion a year worldwide, a figure which is only going to rise in the coming years.

The industry is home to many different occupations and employs hundreds of thousands around the world.

Video games can cost as much to produce as major Hollywood movies – and can earn much more. 2014's *Destiny*, for instance, cost $500 million to develop – twice as much as any film made that year. But apparently, following its release, the game made that money back in just one day!

Yet many still see gaming as child's play, and the industry still struggles to be taken seriously. With over 1.2 billion people now playing games, 700 million of them online, perhaps it's time to reconsider our ideas of who gamers are and why they spend so much time and money on their passion.

▶ TRACK 67

Je = Jermaine, Jo = Jodie, Ja = James

Je: Welcome to another Three Jays podcast – *Totally great or Total rubbish?* For those joining us for the first time, me – Jermaine – and my friends James and Jodie review random stuff chosen by listeners and decide if they're totally great or total rubbish. That's it. No maybes – it's all or nothing. You're either grade A or a hopeless fail. So first up, it's me with 'Cry for help', an app to scare off attackers.
OK. Imagine walking home at night. Someone's following you – a robber or worse. You open the app and 'Help!!!' No-one's going to attack you with that screaming in their ear.

Jo: Come on! What's wrong with using your own voice?

Je: You haven't had that dream where you want to scream, but nothing comes out?

Jo: Er, it's a dream, right – not reality.

Ja: They might cover your mouth.

Jo: Or smash your phone.

Ja: True.

Jo: Apart from that, some creep's considering robbing me, right, so I pull out a £500 phone and start searching through my apps! You don't think he might be more tempted to rob me?

Ja: She has a point.

Jo: It's rubbish.

Je: Good for scaring your little brother, though ... 'Help!!!'

Ja: No maybes. Total rubbish.

Je: OK, a hopeless fail. So, James, what about your 'Universal Translator'?

Ja: Yeah, basically, it's an app that allows you to speak in a foreign language you don't know. You just say the words in English and the app plays a spoken translation with the correct accent.

Jo: Wow. Sounds cool. Having something like that on your travels has to be good, no?

Ja: It's good in theory, but it's difficult to know if the translation is accurate, so I asked a Chinese friend to try it out with me.

Je: Ha! Any good?

Ja: Well, some were OK – like 'Hello', 'Goodbye', 'Can I have a coffee?' Stuff like that.

Jo: Cool.

Ja: But I did try and say 'Your mum's nice' and, apparently, it said 'I like your cow.'

Je: Ha ha! Dude, I'm not sure what's more embarrassing – the translation or saying your mate's mum is 'nice'.

Ja: She made us cookies.

Je: OK.

Jo: Whatever. What about the other way round?

Ja: Oh, it only recognises English at the moment.

Jo: So you ask the way to the bank, but you can't follow the directions. Hardly a universal translator!

Ja: True. But it is half the problem sorted in twelve languages. And the other people could point. They might even take you there.

Je: And if they try and attack you on the way it could translate this – 'Help!!!'

Ja: Exactly.

Je: Saves you having to learn a language.

Ja: I'd say it's totally great.

Jo: OK, you win.

Je: Universal Translator we are agreed you are totally great. Which brings us to Jodie and the 'Remote Lock'.

Jo: So you install this lock, and then you can use the app on your phone to lock or unlock it from anywhere – Australia if you wanted to!

Ja: Why on earth would you want to open a door from the other side of the world?

Jo: Well ...

▶ **TRACK 68**

1 I need it to fix this with.
2 You should've told me.
3 You shouldn't have done that.
4 If I'd known, I could've done something about it.
5 Being the boss's daughter made working there quite hard.
6 I'm really looking forward to seeing you all again.

UNIT 15

▶ **TRACK 69**

1

A: Hello. Mr Gomez?

B: Yes?

A: I'm sorry. Have you been waiting long?

B: About two hours.

A: I'm sorry, we're quite busy today. You've done something to your ankle?

B: Yes.

A: Hmm, it's quite swollen. Does this hurt?

B: Yeah, it's very painful.

A: Can you put any weight on it at all?

B: No, no. It hurts too much.

A: Hmm. And how did you do it?

B: I was just coming out of the hotel and I slipped on the stair and my ankle … it just …

A: You just fell over on it. Nasty. Well, I think we should do an X-ray. It might just be badly sprained, but it could be broken. You'll have to wait again, I'm afraid. We've been a bit short of staff lately. I'll ask the nurse to give you something for the pain.

B: Good. How long will I have to wait for the X-ray?

A: Hopefully, it won't be more than half an hour. Are you on any medication?

B: Er … I take something for my asthma.

A: That's fine. Have you ever had any adverse reactions to any painkillers – paracetamol or anything?

B: No, never.

A: OK, fine. Well, I'll get the nurse to give you something and then take you down for the X-ray.

2

C: Hello.

D: Hello.

E: Hello.

C: Take a seat. What seems to be the problem?

D: It's my boyfriend. He's been up all night throwing up. He's hardly slept, he had a high temperature – 39 – and his heart was beating really fast.

C: And how long have you been like this?

D: Sorry, he doesn't speak much English. He first said he felt a bit sick yesterday afternoon and then he threw up about seven and he hasn't really stopped since.

C: Oh dear. Any diarrhoea?

D: Actually, no, none.

C: And has he been able to drink anything?

D: No, that's the problem. When he drinks water, he's sick again.

C: Right, well, let's have a look. Can you just take off your jumper and sit up here? Open your mouth and stick your tongue out. Lovely. And now take a deep breath. Again … breathe in … and out. Just lie down. I'm going to press quite hard. Does it hurt? And here?

E: Hmm. It's OK.

C: Maybe a bit uncomfortable – but no pain?

E: Yes … no pain.

C: OK, you can put your jumper back on. I think it's viral gastroenteritis, so there's no need for antibiotics. I'll give him an injection to stop the vomiting and then he just needs to rest and take lots of fluids. OK. Any questions?

D: No, I don't think so. I'll explain to him.

▶ **TRACK 70**

A = Anna, D = Dan

A: How was your holiday? You went mountain biking in Austria, didn't you?

D: That's right. It was great, except for James's accident.

A: Why? What happened?

D: Well, we'd been cycling in the mountains round Kaunertal, and we were going back to the hotel down this steep road. James went round this tight bend too fast and he went off the road into some bushes and fell off. It was horrible.

A: It sounds it! Was he badly hurt?

D: Well, we thought so. We were worried that he'd maybe hit his head because he kept asking us where he was and what had happened. He just seemed really confused. At one point, actually, he even asked if we'd met somewhere before!

A: Really?

D: Yeah, and we could see that his knee was very swollen as well. He also had quite a few cuts and bruises and was bleeding quite a bit. The problem was, though, we were still miles from the next village.

A: So, what happened? How did you get him to a hospital?

D: Well, luckily, we were actually on a road and a car came past a minute or two later. It stopped and the woman driving said she'd take James to the nearest hospital. He kept saying he'd be OK, but she insisted and in the end we managed to get him to go – just to be safe. We got him into the car and she took my mobile number and promised to call me once there was more news.

A: Wow! That was nice.

D: I know. It was really kind of her. Anyway, we then cycled back to our hotel and waited to hear from the hospital.

A: And did they call?

D: Yeah, they did. After a couple of hours, they rang and told me they'd given James an X-ray and there was nothing broken and nothing wrong with his head. But they said he needed to stay there a bit longer, as he was waiting to have a few stitches in the cuts.

A: Oh, poor guy!

D: Yeah, I know. In the end, he spent the rest of the holiday hanging around the hotel. He was desperate to go out with us, but the doctors told him not to cycle for a week and to rest the knee. It spoilt his holiday really.

A: I bet!

D: And, on top of all that, I spoke to him yesterday and he said he's going to have to buy a new bike now because of the accident. He's found out the bike frame's broken.

A: Ouch! That actually reminds me of something that happened to some friends of mine when they went camping in Croatia …

UNIT 16

1

A: Did you see that thing in the paper about Shaynee Wilson?

B: No. What was that?

A: Well, you remember she got married last September, right?

B: Yeah, they were at that film premiere recently. He's that short blonde guy.

A: Exactly. Well, she's just announced they're splitting up!

B: Wow, that didn't last long, did it?

A: Apparently, she found out that he's having an affair with some other Hollywood actress.

B: So, did he get much of her money?

2

C: Did you see that thing on the Times website about the steel plant closing down?

D: You're joking! Doesn't your friend Jim work there?

C: Yeah. I haven't spoken to him yet.

D: So how come it's being shut down? Has the company gone bankrupt?

C: No! Apparently they're doing quite well. They even promised to expand last year.

D: So how come ...?

C: The usual – it was taken over and the new management claim it's too expensive to run. They're moving production abroad.

D: That's terrible! So how many people are going to lose their jobs?

3

E: Did you see that thing on TV about that murder in town?

F: Yeah, shocking, isn't it? How can someone stab someone to death in a crowded place like that in the middle of the day and then get away?

F: I know.

E: Apparently, no-one offered to help the victim or did anything to stop the guy who did it.

F: It is bad, but then again, what would you have done?

4

G: Have you heard the news?

H: No. What?

G: The deputy president's resigned.

H: Really? Why's that?

G: Haven't you been following the story? He's been accused of doing all kinds of things. Like apparently, he took illegal payments connected to that new national sports stadium.

H: Right.

G: Not that he's admitted to doing anything. He just apologised for 'causing the government difficulties'.

H: Right. So what else has he been accused of?

5

I: Did you see that thing in the paper about Real Madrid wanting to sign Geraldinho?

J: I know. It's bad news for our team, isn't it? Apparently, he's refused to play in any friendly matches before the start of the season.

I: Well, that's that then! This is going to be a terrible season. We needed to buy a top midfielder, not sell one!

J: Well, Real are supposed to be offering 40 million, which will help.

I: Maybe. But who are we going to get to replace him?

1

A: Have you seen that thing on Twitter about that tennis player, James Jenkins?

B: Yeah, what an idiot. Apparently, it's been retweeted a million times already.

2

A: Have you seen that video on YouTube of the prime minister trying to dance to hip-hop?

B: Yeah, it's so funny, isn't it? Apparently, it was from before he went into politics, though.

3

A: Did you see that thing on TV about them building a new airport?

B: Yeah, it's good news, isn't it? Apparently, it's going to create 1,000 jobs.

4

A: Did you see that thing on the news about the murder near here last night?

B: Yeah, it's awful, isn't it? Apparently, the victim was quite young.

5

A: Did you see that thing on the Times website about Shaynee Wilson getting arrested?

B: Yeah, it's sad, isn't it? The media are obsessed with that woman.

1

A: Who's the statue of?

B: That's Garibaldi.

A: Garibaldi?

B: You've never heard of him?

A: No, I don't think so. Who was he?

B: He was a military leader in the nineteenth century who helped unify Italy. He's like a national hero. He fought in South America as well. He was part of the liberation struggles in Brazil and Uruguay. I think his first wife was even Brazilian. I'm surprised you haven't heard of him.

A: Well, I'm not really interested in history.

2

C: You've been away, haven't you?

D: Yeah, I went to Germany as part of a Comenius project.

C: Comenius project?

D: Yeah, it's a European Union scheme which provides grants to teachers so that they can go on courses or set up partnerships with other schools abroad.

C: Sounds interesting. I've never heard of it. Why Comenius then? What does that mean?

D: He was a Czech writer who wrote about education. Apparently, he's seen as the father of modern education.

C: Oh yeah? I've never heard of him.

D: Well, to be honest, neither had I before I went on this course. He sounds incredible, though. He was writing in the seventeenth century, but even then he was arguing for education for both boys and girls.

C: Really? Wow! That was very radical.

D: Yeah, and he was against just learning by heart, you know. He wanted kids to learn by actually doing things and he encouraged them to think for themselves. He was really ahead of his time.

C: He sounds it.

3

E: So what are you going to do while you're in Brussels?

F: Work mainly, but I'm hoping to go to the Eddy Merckx metro station while I'm there.

E: Really? Why do you want to go there?

F: It's where they have Eddy Merckx's bike, which he used to set the hour record.

E: What? What are you talking about?

F: Eddy Merckx? He's like the greatest cyclist of all time! They named the metro station after him and it has all kinds of memorabilia there.

E: Oh right.

F: You've never heard of him?

E: Er … no. And you're not planning to go anywhere else, like the Magritte Museum?

F: Magritte?

E: The surrealist painter. He was the guy that did pictures of office workers raining down from the sky.

F: It doesn't sound familiar.

E: 'Ceci n'est pas une pipe?'

F: Sorry, you've lost me.

E: You must know it! It's one of his paintings. It's a picture of a pipe and underneath it says, 'This is not a pipe' in French. You'd recognise it if you saw it. It's really famous.

F: Yeah, well, so is Eddy Merckx, but you didn't know him!

REVIEW 8

▶ **TRACK 74**

1 I've been under a lot of stress lately.
2 Hopefully, it's just an upset stomach.
3 They asked if I was allergic to anything.
4 He's never apologised for saying what he said.
5 It didn't happen during the time that I worked there.
6 She's been accused of stealing money at work.

NATIONAL GEOGRAPHIC LEARNING | CENGAGE Learning

Outcomes Intermediate
Student's Book Split B
Hugh Dellar and Andrew Walkley

Publisher: Gavin McLean

Publishing Consultant: Karen Spiller

Development Editor: Katy Wright

Editorial Manager: Claire Merchant

Head of Strategic Marketing ELT: Charlotte Ellis

Senior Content Project Manager: Nick Ventullo

Senior Production Controller: Eyvett Davis

Cover design: emc design

Text design: Alex Dull

Compositor: emc design

National Geographic Liaison:
    Wesley Della Volla / Leila Hishmeh

Audio: Tom Dick & Debbie Productions Ltd

DVD: Tom Dick & Debbie Productions Ltd

Student's Book Split B ISBN: 978-1-337-56121-1

National Geographic Learning
Cheriton House
North Way
Andover
UK
SP10 5BE

Cengage Learning is a leading provider of customized learning solutions with employees residing in nearly 40 different countries and sales in more than 125 countries around the world. Find your local representative at **www.cengage.com**.

Cengage Learning products are represented in Canada by Nelson Education Ltd.

Visit National Geographic Learning online at **ngl.cengage.com**
Visit our corporate website at **www.cengage.com**

CREDITS

Although every effort has been made to contact copyright holders before publication, this has not always been possible. If contacted, the publisher will undertake to rectify any errors or omissions at the earliest opportunity.

Printed in Greece by Bakis SA
Print Number: 01   Print Year: 2017

Photos

6–7 © Babak Tafreshi/National Geographic Creative; 9 © Radius Images/Corbis; 10 © Qilai Shen/In Pictures/Corbis; 11 © Homer Sykes/Alamy; 12 © NiseriN/Getty Images; 13 (l) © Michael Hanschke/dpa/Corbis; 13 (m) © SeanPavonePh/Getty Images; 13 (r) © Iain Masterton/Alamy; 14–15 © Greg Dale/National Geographic Creative; 16 © Anders Ryman/Corbis; 18 (tl) © Jonathan Irish/ National Geographic Creative; 18 (tr) © Sean Pavone/Shutterstock.com; 18 (bl) © Reza Estakhrian/Getty Images; 18–19 © Arterra Picture Library/Alamy; 19 (br) © John W Banagan/Getty Images; 20–21 © Julian Smith/Corbis; 22 © Franck Guiziou/Corbis; 24–25 © Jeff Topping/Getty Images; 26 © Fendis/Corbis; 27 © Jason Stang/Corbis; 29 (inset) © Keystone-France/Getty Images; 29 © Splash News/Corbis; 30 © Frank and Helen Schreider/National Geographic Creative; 32–33 © Chris Johns/National Geographic Creative; 34 © Alaska Stock Images/National Geographic Creative; 36 © Mika/Corbis; 38–39 © Atlantide Phototravel/Corbis; 40 © Nir Alon/Demotix/Corbis; 42–43 © Jason Edwards/National Geographic Creative; 44 (t) © whitelook/Shutterstock.com; 44 (mt) © Ivonne Wierink/Shutterstock.com; 44 (mb) © Vereshchagin Dmitry/Shutterstock.com; 44 (b) © AlexKZ/Shutterstock.com; 46–47 © STR/Reuters/Corbis; 49 (t) © Richard Baker/In Pictures/Corbis; 49 (b) © Heide Benser/Corbis; 50–51 © f8 Imaging/Hulton Archive/Getty Images; 55 © DOMINICK REUTER/Reuters/Corbis; 56 © Hannibal Hanschke/Reuters; 58 © Maggie Steber/National Geographic Creative; 60–61 © Joel Sartore/National Geographic Creative; 62 © Alex Treadway/National Geographic Creative; 66 (l) © Dylan Ellis/Corbis; 66 (r) © Astrid Gast/Getty Images; 67 (l) © Mattias Klum/Corbis; 67 (r) © Rebecca Drobis/Corbis; 68–69 © Wim Wiskerke/Alamy; 70 © Mike Theiss/National Geographic Creative; 72 (l) © Bettmann/Corbis; 72 (r) © Photos.com/ Getty Images; 73 (tl) © Toni Albir/epa/Corbis; 73 (tr) © Photos.com/Getty Images; 73 (bl) © Louise Gubb/CORBIS SABA; 73 (br) © adoc-photos/Corbis; 74 © Web Pix/Alamy; 75 (l) © Kalyan Chakravorty/The India Today Group/Getty Images; 75 (r) © Alexander Hassenstein/Getty Images; 76 © Lynn Johnson/National Geographic Creative; 78 (t) © Joan Cros Garcia/Demotix/Corbis; 78 (b) © amedved/Getty Images; 80 (tl) © Amy Toensing/National Geographic Society/Corbis; 80 (tr) © Wolfgang Kaehler/Getty Images; 80 (bl) © Jupiterimages/Getty Images; 80 (br) © Jodie Griggs/Getty Images; 81 (t) © Katarina Premfors/Getty Images; 81 (b) © Ragnar Schmuck/Corbis; 83 © Joel Sartore/National Geographic Creative; 85 (t) © AF archive/Alamy; 85 (m) © Moviestore collection Ltd/Alamy; 85 (b) © Pictorial Press Ltd/Alamy; 98 (tl) © Eric Isselee/Shutterstock.com; 98 (tml) © MetaTools; 98 (tmr) © Iakov Filimonov/Shutterstock.com; 98 (tr) © SuperStock; 98 (mtl) © SuperStock; 98 (mtml) © anat chant/Shutterstock.com; 98 (mtmr) © Jules Frazier/Getty Images; 98 (mtr) © TAGSTOCK1/Shutterstock.com; 98 (mbl) © SuperStock; 98 (mbml) © Eric Isselee/ Shutterstock.com; 98 (mbmr) © SuperStock; 98 (mbr) © Ingram Publishing/SuperStock; 98 (bl) © Ingram Publishing/SuperStock; 98 (bm) © SuperStock; 98 (br) © photolinc/Shutterstock.com.

Cover
Cover photograph © Mauricio Abreu/JAI/Corbis.

Illustrations
8 Phil Hackett/Eye Candy; 17 Sarah Knight; 52 Phil Hackett/Eye Candy; 65 David Litchfield/Bright Agency.

Video
(Florence) © Gurgen Bakhshetsyan/Shutterstock.com; (Bejing) © Assawin/Getty Images; (Cordoba) © wavipicture/Getty Images; (Jeju) © Douglas MacDonald/Getty Images; (Alaska) © Tony Waltham/Getty Images; (Lake Baikal) © Nutexzles/Getty Images; (Rapa Nui/Easter Island) © Jim Richardson/Getty Images; (River Rheine) © Heinz Wohner/LOOK-foto/Getty Images; (Cappadocia) © dziewul/Getty Images; (The Leaning Tower of Pisa) © O. LOUIS MAZZATENTA/National Geographic Creative; (Machu Pichu) © Vladislav T. Jirousek/Shutterstock.com; (Mount Kilimanjaro)© invisiblewl/Getty Images.

Text
We are grateful to the following for permission to reproduce copyright material:
National Geographic for text based on the video Cultural Sensitivity, 5844.flv, http://netpub.ngsp.com/netpub/server. np?find&site=Video_NG_01_PUB&catalog=catalog&template=detail.np&field=itemid&op=matches&value=233521, copyright © 2013, National Geographic Channel. Reproduced with permission; Mr Nicholas Wood for a quotation. Reproduced with kind permission of Mr Nicholas Wood, Political Tours, http://www.politicaltours.com; and Mr James Willcox for a quotation as published in Vacations in Dangerous Places by David Peisner, Departures, 22 August 2012. Reproduced with kind permission of Mr James Willcox, Untamed Borders Ltd, www.untamedborders.com.

Acknowledgements
The publisher and authors would like to thank the following teachers who provided the feedback and user insights on the first edition of Outcomes that have helped us develop this new edition:
Rosetta d'Agostino, New English Teaching, Milan, Italy; Victor Manuel Alarcón, EOI Badalona, Badalona, Spain; Isidro Almendarez, Universidad Complutense, Madrid, Spain; Isabel Andrés, EOI Valdemoro, Madrid, Spain; Brian Brennan, International House Company Training, Barcelona, Spain; Nara Carlini, Università Cattolica, Milan, Italy; Karen Corne, UK; Jordi Dalmau, EOI Reus, Reus, Spain; Matthew Ellman, British Council, Malaysia; Clara Espelt, EOI Maresme, Barcelona, Spain; Abigail Fulbrook, Chiba, Japan; Dylan Gates, Granada, Spain; Blanca Gozalo, EOI Fuenlabrada, Madrid, Spain; James Grant, Japan; Joanna Faith Habershon, St Giles Schools of Languages London Central, UK; Jeanine Hack; English Language Coach.com, London, UK; Claire Hart, Germany; David Hicks, Languages4Life, Barcelona, Spain; Hilary Irving, Central School of English, London, UK; Jessica Jacobs, Università Commerciale Luigi Bocconi, Milan, Italy; Lucia Luciani, Centro di Formaziones Casati, Milan, Italy; Izabela Michalak, ELC, Łódź, Poland; Josep Millanes Moya, FIAC Escola d'Idiomes, Terrassa, Catalonia; Rodrigo Alonso Páramo, EOI Viladecans, Barcelona, Spain; Jonathan Parish, Uxbridge College, London, UK; Mercè Falcó Pegueroles, EOI Tortosa, Tortosa, Spain; Hugh Podmore, St Giles Schools of Languages London Central, UK; James Rock, Università Cattolica, Milan, Italy; Virginia Ron, EOI Rivas, Madrid, Spain; Coletto Russo, British Institutes, Milan, Italy; Ana Salvador, EOI Fuenlabrada, Madrid, Spain; Adam Scott, St Giles College, Brighton, UK; Olga Smolenskaya, Russia; Carla Stroulger, American Language Academy, Madrid, Spain; Simon Thomas, St Giles, UK; Simon Thorley, British Council, Madrid, Spain; Helen Tooke, Università Commerciale Luigi Bocconi, Milan, Italy; Chloe Turner, St Giles Schools of Languages London Central, UK; Sheila Vine, University of Paderborn, Germany; Richard Willmsen, British Study Centres, London, UK; Various teachers at English Studio Academic management, UK.

Authors' acknowledgements
Thanks to Karen Spiller and Katy Wright, and to Dennis Hogan, John McHugh and Gavin McLean for their continued support and enthusiasm.
Thanks also to all the students we've taught over the years for providing more inspiration and insight than they ever realised.
And to the colleagues we've taught alongside for their friendship, thoughts and assistance.